RETHINK READING STRATEGIES

Teaching Children with Learning Differences to Read in 14 Days, *Really!*

© 2015 by Suki Stone, PhD
Second Edition

Stonebridge Academic Publishing
San Diego, California

ISBN-978-0-9861147-0-0

DISCLAIMER: The contents of this publication are intended for educational and informative use only and not to be considered a directive nor a guide to self-diagnosis or self-treatment.

Cover and Interior Design by Victoria Vinton

i

Enjoy the book,

Call Me !

2017

Suki Stone wants to get America reading, and parents and teachers should start with this fascinating, valuable book that could get kids away from television and back to reading books. Of course, this is bad news for TV writers like me. My four siblings are all teachers, and they're each getting a copy of this important book for Christmas.

— **Mike Reiss**
Emmy-winning Writer/Producer *"The Simpsons"*

The pages of Dr. Stone's wise and caring *Rethink Reading Strategies* glow with the author's passion to change the world, one child at a time.

— **Richard Lederer, Ph.D.**
Author of *The Gift of Age* **and** *A Tribute to Teachers*

Rethink Reading Strategies – do it now! The answer already lies within your child...their own personal knowledge will unlock their reading potential. Rethink your child's reading strategies; let Dr. Stone show you how!

— **Don Brown**
Author of *Bring Out the Best in Every Employee* **and** *What Got You Here Won't Get You There in Sales*

Acknowledgments

I want to acknowledge my family for their constant support and love, especially my brothers Richard and Robert, who supported the vision of my life's work as I engaged in writing this book. Pat Tannagon, my colleague for thirty years, first suggested many years ago that I needed to write a book. She said it was important to tell my story so that all children could benefit from knowing help was available for them to succeed. Pat has been a special friend who really saw how much I cared for every child to have the potential to read. She has always been an inspiration to me. I want to thank my friend and colleague Deborah Storton, a school speech therapist, who was always encouraging me to write this book. We shared teaching some of the same children, and she believed my writing a book would send the message that parents and teachers need to recognize and acknowledge their children were truly smart. Julie Johnson-Berg, my colleague, helped me realize that the children's voices were important and that they needed the recognition they deserved. Julie championed my efforts and vision with positive encouragement. I want to thank Dr. Alice Quiocho, who became my mentor as I took steps to help other teachers. She gave me the opportunity to speak about new approaches to teaching reading in her university classes and set the stage for my program to be used in teacher training.

My colleague, Jacquie Montegue, gave her special education students an opportunity to improve their reading skills with my program **You Read**. Those experiences provided the scenarios for this book. I am truly grateful for Jacquie's faith and trust that would enable her students to become grade-level readers. I want to thank my colleague and friend, Dr. Unoma Comer, who reassured me that this was truly the time to write about new ways to teach children with learning disabilities to read. She reinforced my recognition that children had learning differences, not disabilities. Dr. Etta Baldwin, a supervisor of district libraries in Greensboro, North Carolina, believed it was necessary to discuss core standards for reading regarding children with learning disabilities. The chapter entitled "Skill Development Begins with the Child, Not the Reading Skills" was her suggestion. I am grateful to Dr. James Jaurez, who encouraged me to use the computer as a new tool for **You Read**. He knew there was a way writing tablets could enhance my process. A special thank you goes to Dr. Albert Cruz and his student, Emily Choi.

With their extensive experience and knowledge of information technology, they provided the research material on the importance of using technology for children with learning disabilities. This was important in understanding how technology is definitely an asset for improving literacy skills. To Liz Goodgold, my faithful marketing sage, I am truly grateful for her coaching, recommendations, and conviction in knowing that I needed to share my knowledge and my work to help children and give them a voice.

I want to recognize Alan Townsend, who has a great love for my reading-challenged children and recognizes them personally when they succeed. He and his staff have helped me by providing a teaching space. A thank you to my good friends Wendy Vaughn, Steve Hostetler, Shirley Ginsberg, and Miriam Plotkin, who saw me through the times I questioned whether I had anything to say that would fill the pages for a book. A special thank you to Shirley for the first edits and to Victoria Vinton who greatly assisted with the publication. Their knowledge and experience made the printed words a reality.

I owe a special thank you to all the children who have successfully completed my program. Their parents and grandparents wanted to make sure they had the best chance to succeed.

Dedication

This book is dedicated to my parents, Millie and Sheldon Stone, who knew I had something to share with children and encouraged me to never give up on my mission. Their support and love have always been the light that shines in my life.

Preface

Rethink Reading Strategies is written for parents who see their children struggle with reading and writing skills and to help parents and teachers realize their children can truly learn and achieve at their highest potential by changing how they think about themselves. This change begins with the fact that they need to be referred to as children with learning *differences*, not learning disabilities. The famous people we hear about— Albert Einstein, Richard Branson, Steven Spielberg, Orlando Bloom, Cher, and Jay Leno—refer to themselves as having dyslexia or learning disabilities, but they are really extraordinary people who learn differently. This book is about acknowledging children's differences as strengths and changing the way we, as parents and teachers, *refer to these children*, treat, and teach them. The premise identifies children as being able to be our teachers, looks at a new standard and theory about how to teach children with disabilities, and accepts the children for what they *can* do rather than try and *fix* what they can't do. Although children in the book are referred to as having learning disabilities, dyslexia, attention deficit disorder (ADD), or attention deficit hyperactivity disorder (ADHD), and have been given these "labels," they are really children who have different ways of learning. The term "learning disabilities" will be used throughout the book to represent those labels. Join me in this new journey to recognize children for their strengths, talents, and creativity, while learning how to provide the support, encouragement, and foundation for children's success.

Contents

Chapter 1

What Needs to Change in the Teaching of Reading

Roger was a high school senior. He was large in stature and was covered with tattoos. Initially, I wasn't comfortable around Roger—he frightened me. The tattoos and his stature were intimidating. He was a student in a special education resource room and was academically failing in his major subject areas, except recess and lunch. He had been in special education classes since fourth grade, but teachers told him he would never advance beyond reading at the first-grade level. I approached him just like any one of my school children who knew they were smart, but couldn't read.

I was confident that I could teach Roger, and I wanted him to understand that he had the ability to succeed. I told Roger he would learn to read proficiently and pass all his classes in his last year of high school. He was puzzled because I had no books or workbooks to use with him. I explained that his life experiences were the basis for teaching him reading skills and asked him to share what he considered his passions. The first idea he shared was his love for raising his pot belly pig. (I was fascinated that he was raising a pig; it is not something I hear every day.)

As an authentic teacher/mentor, I needed to make sure Roger knew my sincerity when I asked him, "You're raising a what? You like raising a pig?" He laughed and said, "You're going to teach me to read by my telling you about raising a pot belly pig?" I replied emphatically, "Yes! You have all the knowledge you need now to get started."

We proceeded with the process and his reading improved to such a degree that he received A's and one B in all classes related to his language and literacy skills for his last semester of classes in high school.

If changes were made in the current educational system, children who are failing would have a chance to actually become successful readers. But first, we need to look at what needs to change.

We can conclude that if new assumptions about reading were made in the current system, children who are failing might have a chance to actually become successful readers. First, we need to understand how reading has traditionally been taught. Then we will question what we know or *think* we know about children—as well as reading—in order to develop a new set of assumptions. The problem children with learning disabilities face in our schools are the traditional ways in which reading is taught. Schools and the people in charge of curricula believe in their fallacy for learning, which is the rationale that when children are not learning the structure of how to read, they require more time and more intensive work using the same process. (This is analogous to speaking louder when talking to someone who doesn't speak your language, thinking that volume will compensate for understanding.) Reading is a complex skill, but doesn't need to be that complicated. When we look at teaching reading from a different paradigm, it will cease to be an overwhelming task. Then we will apply a different set of assumptions and track the development of a new paradigm. **A paradigm is a set of assumptions that we believe forms our practice. A paradigm is not a method or a way of executing practice. It is similar to beliefs and values.** So let's get started.

The Real Reason We Read

The *real* reason we read is to comprehend information. Learning new vocabulary, writing, and spelling are taught in various sequences, but these are usually taught *after* teaching letter combinations and sounds. The traditional approach is to teach parts of the process and progress to learning the whole of reading rather than teaching the process of literacy as a total process, which integrates all the components. The method of teaching parts that eventually should be used to help children see and read the whole word doesn't make sense for learning disabled children.

Children have different learning styles, and while most children understand the relationship with letters and sounds, children with learning disabilities have difficulty distinguishing between sounds and the changes that are made to read different words. We fail to tell children that the words in the English language are from various European countries, so when sounds have a certain pattern, but the pattern isn't consistent, the children are unable to remember and retain the words. Teachers are taught to teach exceptions, but there are so many exceptions in the English language that children get confused. Children with learning disabilities are more likely to be visual learners. Although schools talk about teaching reading as a balanced approach, teachers still begin the process of teaching sounds using an auditory method.

How Reading is Currently Taught

Reading has been taught for decades and is currently taught by learning the letter combinations and sounds. The teaching of reading for teachers is usually introduced in university education methods courses. Consequently, teachers use these universal methods the same way. There is a systematic way each letter sound is learned. The 26 letters of the English alphabet are not always learned in order, but most often teachers begin with teaching the letter "B." Often consonants are taught first because most words begin with consonants and are easier to pronounce. As children learn each consonant letter, and its corresponding sound, the objective for reading words is to couple the letters together for three-letter words. Vowels are taught in order of the alphabet because the letter "a" when coupled with the letter "b" can make a word. Children write the letters and then learn that letter combinations like "cab" "can" "cap" "car" and "cat" are words. So the teaching of reading encompasses three letter words first. After these combinations have been mastered (many children with learning disabilities can't master sounds), the children learn that these sounds form words.

Publishing companies produce many programs with subtle changes, but they are usually structured in the same format. First, children learn the letters of the alphabet and what sounds are associated with those letters. These pre-reading skills are referred to as phonemic awareness. Then they learn how the various sounds which are put together make words, and learn to pronounce those words based on the combination of sounds. This process is usually referred to as phonics. The system of phonics recognizes that word forms are predictable. For example, when children learn the sound of the letter "o" in a word, they may believe that the combinations are pronounced the same way in other words as well. However, not all letters maintain the same sounds, so there is much confusion as to which words actually are pronounced the same. For example, hope and rope are pronounced the same, but not love and move, even though they have the same three letters in the same sequence. Children who learn phonics well and are very successful in pronouncing words become "word callers" because they do not consistently know what the words mean. They can read almost any word, even if it is a made up word because they recognize the structure of the phonemes.

Some children learn very quickly and other children can't "get the picture." The problem that children with learning disabilities face in our schools is understanding the traditional teaching of reading. School curricula are based on various educational philosophies for learning. One specific philosophy when children are not learning how to read is the assumption that they require more time and more intensive work using the same process. More time with the same technique will not change the results. A change in the approach and technique needs to be made to change the responses of children with learning problems.

Change the set of assumptions and we change our thinking. Children need a new way to think about how they learn to read.

I am not opposed to phonics as an approach to literacy and learning to read. It works for most children, and is a very successful method. The specifics of learning words and their pronunciations are best taught between kindergarten and third grade. Those are the years that children are most flexible and open to understanding the parts and essentials of the phonemes, which are the smallest basic unit of language. Letters are phonemes that when put together make words. Whether the letters are vowels or consonants, they are designated as phonemes. Since the English language is a combination of many other languages, we have letter combinations that are not always consistent. Some phonemes have different sounds when they are combined with different letters. Most children can differentiate between those sounds. It is important to understand that the process of learning phonics requires children to understand the subtle differences and be able to follow the examples that present those differences. It is also important for teachers to emphasize that those differences give children a chance to practice words already in their vocabulary, so they know how those differences apply to words they use.

Phonics is Appropriate for Most Children

It is important to note that phonics, as a structural process and technique to teach literacy skills, is suitable for most children. The system has been an effective approach to learning to read. The theory behind the teaching of phonics is that children can't learn to read sufficiently unless they are taught how the individual letters and sounds form words, and how words together create sentences. The philosophy of learning to read is that reading can't be taught without children learning sounds and being able to differentiate sounds within the words. Additionally, it is understood and accepted that once children learn words and are able to sound out words in a sentence, they consider this reading. Learning to read words is the beginning of reading or literacy training. However, the generally accepted method of teaching reading is the teaching of phonics.

When children with learning disabilities have had phonics lessons and classes for many years and are still not progressing at the rate of their peers, it might be advantageous to find another approach to teach them to read. When children are not progressing because of learning problems, many people who embrace phonics also include supplemental materials and use the term "a balanced approach to reading." When people refer to a balanced reading program they are acknowledging that phonics and whole language are taught together. Since the research doesn't specify to what degree each approach is to be emphasized, it is at the teacher's discretion how much time he or she decides to spend on each approach. However, even when a teacher introduces whole language into the reading instruction, phonics is usually taught before whole language instruction. Sometimes introducing a balanced program helps children with learning disabilities read proficiently. The research on a balanced program has acknowledged helping children from falling behind.

Even by combining phonics and whole language, it may still be difficult for children with learning disabilities to read proficiently. After years of trying to teach children with learning disabilities, even with a balanced approach, it may be time to change the way we structure reading instruction that is neither phonics nor whole language. As we change and adopt a new structure, we change the paradigm.

Why Phonics Doesn't Work
for Some Learning Disabled Children

One of the main reasons phonics doesn't work for children with learning disabilities is that they have difficulty distinguishing between letter sounds. The term that teachers use is "sound or auditory discrimination." Children with learning disabilities have difficulty hearing the differences in various vowel sounds. They can't hear differences in long and short vowels, and there are so many rules to decide whether the vowels in the words are long or short that they continually mispronounce words. A student who is an auditory learner has no problem with hearing the sounds and pronouncing the words.

Children with learning disabilities are unable to retain the information—told to them many times—how the sounds are different. The retention of sounds is not related to any problems with memory. The fact that there are so many rules to follow and so many words that don't adhere to those rules presents a problem to these children. Changes in letter sounds as presented in different words also become a problem. For example, the words *love* and *move* have the same vowels in the same order, but the letter "o" has a different sound in each word. Children with learning disabilities have problems determining how those words are pronounced. They would rather look for word patterns and memorize the words that don't have those patterns. Therefore, they need to learn to read using more visual cues. Although phonics may include using visual cues, the structure of phonics instruction is auditory and uses sounds and sound combinations to teach reading.

What Needs to Change in the Teaching of Reading

The old assumptions that children come to school with an empty slate or total lack of knowledge is a false assumption. Therefore, teaching reading requires a new set of assumptions, and teaching children with learning disabilities to read is a daunting task. For decades, school systems have tried all kinds of processes, methods, and programs and still **have not been able to teach learning disabled children to read with a modicum of success. The reason: they are using the wrong paradigm and don't understand what changes need to be made.** Reading is a complex skill; however, children's prior knowledge increases their ability to acquire reading skills. If reading were taught using a different paradigm, then learning to read would cease to be an overwhelming task.

Turning the Paradigm Upside Down

As I discuss the changes that need to be made in the belief about education as well as reading, it is important to understand that new approaches or methods do not necessarily equal a new paradigm.

When we follow lessons learned and look at each child as an individual, we also look at a different paradigm. **A paradigm is a set of assumptions that we believe forms our practice. A paradigm is not a method or a way of executing practice. It is similar to beliefs and values.** For example, one view currently accepted for teaching disabled children is that everything must be taught in small increments and learned as separate parts. This paradigm of reducing skills to the smallest detail has not worked for children with learning problems.

Changing the paradigm means considering a new belief about how children learn and providing them with strategies that mirror those new beliefs.

When the special education law, Public Law 94-142 Education for All Handicapped Children's Act (PL94-142) was enacted in 1973, the plan was to help children overcome their learning disabilities and read at grade-level standards. Thirty-eight years later, more children are receiving the label of learning disabled and not receiving successful instruction to become proficient readers. According to my experience, the paradigm that educators are still promoting is the problem. Based on the current belief systems educators and legislators have regarding how children are taught to read, their current paradigm *needs* to change. Unless educational decision makers change their belief about how children with learning disabilities are taught, children will not be able to read.

In 2004, the Individuals with Disabilities Education Act (IDEA) was renamed the Individuals with Disabilities Education Improvement Act (IDEIA). The word "improvement" was added because legislators believed children with learning disabilities were receiving skills that improved their abilities to read. If this were truly the case, we wouldn't still have statistics reported by the National Assessment of Educational Progress (NAEP) that found approximately 38 percent of fourth-grade students have "below basic" reading skills. In addition, it is reported that people with poor reading skills are likely to be 70-80 percent dyslexic. The National Center for Educational Statistics (NCES) has reported in 2013, that 80 percent of African American and Hispanic children and 50 percent of white children are reading below basic levels or "Chronically-Below-Basic" levels. These staggering statistics cannot change without embracing a new paradigm.

We are still in need of change based on the current reading statistics. We need to look for another way to approach children with reading disabilities.

When I set out to develop a new approach, I first had to change my own paradigm. I had the same background knowledge as other teachers and used the same exercises for teaching children to read. But I also knew that my techniques were not working and children were not improving. The major difference between me and other educators was that I was a risk taker and prepared to fight for children with learning disabilities. I recognized these children were not credited for their full potential and intuitively I knew their knowledge could help them learn to read. I had discussions with my students and they shared information from their experiences. These experiences were authentic, and students were excited to talk about themselves. They were also excited to teach me. They knew that when I asked them questions, I really wanted to know the answers. I showed the students I was sincere and their information would teach me something I didn't know. They knew that their knowledge was important for me to learn. I began to listen to the children.

My paradigm began with the assumptions that **it isn't the child who needs changing.** My belief is that all children with learning disabilities can learn to read. I also believe no matter what socio-economic conditions these children and their families are experiencing, they come to school with their own knowledge based upon their personal experiences. Those personal experiences can be the basis for teaching them to read. If they begin with something they know, it will also set the stage for learning new material.

The other assumption in my paradigm is that **skills are not taught. The child is taught.** Consequently, the emphasis is on listening to each child and what he or she believes is important. An aspect of listening to the children provides the reasoning for turning the paradigm upside down. We need to accept that children have facts and ideas to share that are new and exciting. Do not assume you know what your child knows. Approach your child with a new set of assumptions and that *you* are the learner in this process.

As adults we are all teachers, but we are also learners. Be open to learn from your children.

Another philosophy and scrutiny of the new paradigm is that writing comes before children read. The reason writing comes first is because children have a natural sequence of learning. That sequence is an intuitive sense of personal knowledge. Dr. Van Allen[1], an educational researcher, coined a phrase that describes that naturalness. He said, "What you think, you can say; what you say, you can write; and what you write, you can read." This phrase supports a new paradigm where writing is the impetus or foundation for children to learn to read, especially children with learning disabilities. Van Allen was insistent in his belief that what a child knows can be written down and then read. I took those concepts and applied them to the children with learning disabilities because I knew that children in my classes were very bright and had knowledge they could share. Most of the time children are not asked about the knowledge they have, and certainly not asked to share it with others.

Reading is your child's thoughts in the written word.

Why Writing is the Secret to Reading

To understand why writing comes before reading may seem like a complex concept. Keep the premise simple. We understand as parents and teachers that our children know things. They are observant and have intuition about what they see and hear. Children are exposed to many ideas, concepts, situations, and experiences, all of which encompass their lives. Using the ideas, situations, concepts, and experiences as the basis for teaching the reading process makes sense. It acknowledges the children and supports their feelings about themselves. Van Allen's approach is a way to reinforce the children and inform them that their personal knowledge reinforces their self-esteem.

All children *know* things. They need to be recognized for their knowledge. They need to be *supported* for what they know.

The new paradigm begins with the writing process because it credits children with the knowledge and experiences they have. This knowledge and those experiences contribute to their ability to write and read. Children become self-assured while they are working in the

[1]Roach Van Allen, *Language Experiences in Communication*. (Boston, MA: Houghton Mifflin) 1976.

9

program and recognize themselves as knowledgeable. As the example at the beginning of this chapter, Roger told me he felt misunderstood and frustrated because he wasn't recognized for his expertise in raising a pot belly pig. That awareness, if used by his teachers, might have shown a passion in a biology class where he would have had a wealth of knowledge related to raising a pot belly pig. Roger would have been transformed with knowing that his knowledge and expertise in that area was important.

The process begins with writing so that children can see how they can conquer the reading process with something they already know. Writing is also a means of enabling children to see what they know as meaningful information and knowledge. As they watch me write their words on the page their ideas are reinforced.

When children write first, they visualize their oral language as written material. They tell their stories about what is important to them. Realizing that I am interested in having them share what they know, they become more confident and see how they can become proficient readers. Writing, first, helps them see and understand that their own experiences are significant. Students become the teacher and I become the learner. Sharing their stories empowers them, and skills are taught incidentally.

The Need for the Program Now

The program is needed now because there are statistics from the National Assessment of Educational Progress (NAEP) publication reporting the percentage of children in the fourth grade reading below basic levels is unchanged. As previously stated, it is reported that 38 percent of fourth-grade students have "below basic" reading skills. It is also reported by NCES that children in all grade levels overall are chronically below basic levels. These children are not progressing at a rate commensurate with their development in comparison with their peers. Currently, according to the organization Students First, two-thirds of fourth graders are reading below the fourth-grade level.

Having taught in the special education field for over thirty years, I have seen many changes in how we classify and teach children with learning disabilities. We continue using the same teaching method with no apparent changes in the children's reading progress. Procedurally we emphasize phonics and dissect learning into bits and pieces, assuming that is how children can retain information. The **You Read** program is needed now to advance these children with their abilities and treat them not as disabled, but rather as differently abled. However, this program does not accommodate all children. In a regular education class, there are only a small number of children at the bottom of their class, which negates whole-class instruction. The **You Read** program helps children learn individually over a period of two weeks. These lessons increase their skill level, improve their self-esteem, and teach them to be independent thinkers.

The process of acknowledging their strengths and teaching them writing, reading, vocabulary, and spelling skills in a comprehensive program is of utmost urgency. The longer we wait for a program of this design, the more children we are going to lose to the skill development processes currently taught.

Since children with learning disabilities are continuing to fall behind their peers at a steady rate, something new must be introduced *now!*

Parents are in need of another paradigm that recognizes their children's strengths and talents. We need to make some changes in the system now. These children can no longer continue to miss out on their educational endeavors and forfeit their dreams because the current systems used in schools are not working for them. We, as teachers, talk about reflecting on the practices that are not working, but don't seem to know how to make changes. Taking chances on something that does have research or is research based, but not in the mainstream, is what needs to happen now to transform the lives of these children with learning disabilities.

The Program Roots in Proven Scientific Theory

You Read is based on proven scientific theory. The theories are based on the work of researchers in education who developed their educational theories for both special education and non-special education children. Dr. Paulo Freire[2], a Brazilian educator, began to examine why migrant workers in Brazil couldn't read although they were intelligent people. He showed them that knowledge they possessed could serve them as they all worked to become proficient readers. He transformed 450 migrant workers in 45 hours. Dr. Freire's book, *Pedagogy of the Oppressed*, presented some of the concepts he originated.

---

2 Paulo Freire, *Pedagogy of the Oppressed*. (New York, NY: Continuum) 1970.

Another researcher, Silvia Ashton-Warner[3], a New Zealand kindergarten teacher, taught her Maori students to read through the use of their own personal vocabulary. Words of which they were familiar were used as reading material, and each child's words were individualized to their personal association. Although her reading lessons were conducted in a group, they did revolve around individual lessons specific to each child. Ms. Ashton-Warner used the children's vocabulary from home to build their skills. Her book, *Teacher*, was original and inspiring, especially in the 1950s. She called her program organic reading because children used their own words integrated into the reading process. She explained that the vocabulary they were learning must be instinctive and meaningful. The words they chose were an integral part of their life experiences. Sylvia Ashton-Warner was cognizant of the way these children responded emotionally to the words they were learning because of their personal connection to them. Once key words are read, the next step begins—the writing process. Ms. Ashton-Warner emphasized the swiftness of her students' writing because they were writing using words or concepts they knew.

Educational researchers who present innovative concepts should be given the opportunity to share their novel approach or system. Educators may be surprised at how other methods can help children learn.

Dr. Roach Van Allen believed that writing came before reading and that children's thoughts were the impetus to their learning to read. He called his method Language Experience and is known as the originator of the Language Experience Approach (LEA) similar to a naturalistic approach to reading. The most interesting practice of the LEA approach is its use in kindergarten classrooms. After kindergarten the LEA approach is not used as often because it usually helps the emergent readers. Children in first grade are concentrating on the mechanics of the reading process as opposed to utilizing a naturalistic approach to reading, which emphasizes children's personal experiences.

Dr. Van Allen's research showed educators the talents children had and how reading could develop through a different systematic method.

---

[3] Sylvia Ashton-Warner, *Teacher*. (New York, NY: Simon and Schuster) 1963.

When children write or dictate their thoughts, they practice their language as a writing skill and consequently the concept of what one thinks, one can say, and one can write. Therefore, the individual learns to read his or her own words, which have been written. Writing comes *before* reading because the process of thought, which becomes the written word, is a prerequisite to reading.

The process of writing before reading follows the same paradigm, which enables children to learn language. Children are not formally taught to speak. The language they learn is through listening and imitating their parents or adults through integration and association. Van Allen's research showed how learning language was the beginning of speaking and reading. Robert Sweet, Jr., researcher from the National Institutes of Health, studied the language of infants and young children, specifying a child has a 25,000-spoken word vocabulary before reaching five years of age or entering formal schooling. That research is important information for parents and teachers of children with learning disabilities because the assumption is that their learning problems overshadow or interfere with their ability to learn reading skills. When educators use children's language and personal experiences as the impetus for teaching reading skills, there is a relationship that children form with their knowledge of their language written down to be used as reading material.

The Swiss psychologist, Jean Piaget[4], was the first person to research how infants acquire knowledge and language and stressed that future experiences of children are based on their previous experiences. Children's language and exposure contribute to these experiences, as Piaget explained with his creation of the spiral of knowledge structure which integrates past experiences with present exposure to expand children's knowledge base. Therefore, new information is gained by learning and transforming previous information. Dr. Piaget used a generative paradigm of holistic constructivist principles. The principles involved teaching from a whole process that encompassed a child's interests, intuition, self-concept, connectedness with others, and trust. Dr. Freire, Dr. Van Allen, Robert Sweet, Jr., Silvia Ashton-Warner, and Dr. Grace Fernald[5], who have a very solid background of success with learning and teaching of reading from a holistic perspective, became

---

[4] Jean Piaget, *The Construction of Reality in the Child.* (New York: Basic Books) 1954.

[5] Grace Fernald, *Remedial Techniques in Basic School Subjects.* (New York: NY: McGraw Hill) 1943.

the foundation for **You Read**. The program has a foundation in reliable and substantial research that originated in 1952 and verifies the success of children with learning disabilities as a viable and valid teaching system.

The prominent educator integrated into **You Read** is Dr. Grace Fernald. She was an educational psychologist who created the multisensory approach, Visual, Auditory, Kinesthetic, and Tactile (VAKT), to teaching reading and spelling. Her method began with the children's choice of words for spelling, reading, and instruction that used a tactile approach to learning. Using the children's senses, recognition, and visual imagery helped them learn to read. This approach used Fernald's imagery so students would visualize the words they were learning. Fernald is known as creator of using sand trays for her tracing technique. Students repeated the letters in the words—not the sound—and traced all the words writing them several times in the sand. The VAKT method is widely used with special education populations, especially children with learning disabilities.

A parent or an educator's open mind can change the life of a child.

Lessons Learned

- Some students, especially those with learning disabilities, are still not mastering the reading process or learning to read sufficiently to become independent readers.
- Every child has a different learning style. Be cognizant of what the child really needs and be ready to adapt.
- The child isn't the problem. We as teachers and administrators need to take the responsibility in providing the best solution for the children's success, even if that means offering another program.
- Do not dismiss research-proven techniques and methods just because educators are unfamiliar with them or they may be controversial. Methods or programs should not be restricted to what is politically correct. Allow children to be successful regardless of what others believe.
- Listen and be attentive to your children and acknowledge what they know.
- Writing helps children see their own thoughts written down. Writing reinforces their self-concept.
- Urgency is a great motivator for change. We must act now to help learning disabled children succeed.
- Research studies are not considered old or ineffective because they are not presently in vogue. To say yes to a new paradigm instead of dismissing it, shows strength of character. To be open to a new set of values that are worthy of investigation is a sign of empowering children.
- When parents and teachers have an open mind or the willingness to change their mind, the window of opportunity for everyone to learn becomes the lesson.

Summary

This chapter introduced the concepts of why we read, how the current reading system is taught, and why phonics doesn't work effectively with many learning disabled children. It explained the new set of values and beliefs that **You Read** embraces, recreating the paradigm and why writing is taught before reading. The concepts presented emphasized accepting a broader view of teaching reading, which is still narrowly focused on phonics. The current system needs to change and realize children may not be retaining the lessons taught with the phonics approach. We may also need to expand our perspectives of learning and teaching and realize children are teachers, especially in **You Read**. Accepting children's ideas and knowledge without judgment is another aspect of understanding the process and the success of children in a short amount of time. These children have experiences that build upon their abilities to learn to read and the need to be recognized and acknowledged for these abilities. The adults who are teaching children with learning disabilities need to give them center stage and help them see how their background knowledge can provide the foundation for learning skills in reading. In addition, educators and parents need to be aware that steps in **You Read** do, indeed, have roots in research-based theory. Some theories may not be as widely known or as overtly used as the phonics theories, but this doesn't negate their effectiveness. It is important to have an open mind and understand that the paradigm may need to be changed to include—if not totally replace—the present paradigm. It must also be known that **You Read** is used mostly with children in special education who may have learning disabilities.

Chapter 2

What Your Child Will Teach You Will Amaze You

Alex was a sixth-grade student who had not mastered reading throughout his elementary school years. After several years of various tutorial programs, Alex was still extremely frustrated because he couldn't read. Upon entering middle school he was failing many of his classes and wanted to give up. His mother asked if I was available to help him. When the family came to the first session, Alex was very upset he had to try another program that he was sure would fail. I discovered from his family that Alex was an avid baseball fan and played on a community team. I knew he was reluctant to participate in my program, but his interest in baseball was the impetus needed in helping him learn to read. I asked him to give me three chances to help him, similar to a baseball player who has three strikes before he's out. If the program was successful for him after the three sessions, then he had to complete the remaining sessions. He agreed to my proposition and to take a reading test to determine his current reading level.

When we started the stories, he told me about a baseball game in which he scored the most runs. I asked him how he felt about being a major scorer to winning that game. I also asked him how this win had impressed his teammates. We needed to choose a vocabulary word that described his situation. Although he really didn't show an interest at first in the thesaurus, we decided on the word "entourage" to explain how he was followed by his teammates because of the respect they had for him as a player. His favorite word that day was entourage. As we wrote the next story, Alex asked me to find the word we needed in the thesaurus. Alex was being proactive and learning the advantages of new vocabulary as it relates to comprehension. To be sure, I didn't strike out, and he enthusiastically finished the sessions. He was no longer frustrated in middle school, and was successful in completing his academic subjects. I contacted him for an update from his middle school experiences. He was proud of the fact he had achieved honor-roll status for every grade in middle school.

Children who read with me build a trust because of how I respond to them. When you find that spark that sets the child up to *teach*, a different relationship is established. A parent must continue to be *willing to learn* from their child and also be willing to be amazed at their knowledge. However, teachers need to be interested in learning what children know. The child that displays problems could also be a leader for a curriculum activity or recognized for his or her knowledge. In my classroom I appointed those children as resource guides when they exhibited special talents. When I became a supervisor for intern teachers, I suggested they identify children in their classroom with special needs and give them an opportunity to be a resource guide.

Treat your children with the respect they deserve for their knowledge.

Listen to Your Children

Listening to your children takes a particular set of skills. With parents' schedules and the responsibilities imposed today, it is difficult to take the time to pay full attention to your children. Parents also believe they know their children and tend not to ask them what they want, what they like, or what they identify as their strengths. The skills involved in *truly* listening to your children begin with an acknowledgement that you want to learn something new about them. Instead of asking them what they did in school that day, rephrase the question to ask, "What did they teach in school today?" Further, ask them if a student in class taught them anything they didn't know. You will be taking the responsibility from the teacher to see if your children recognize anyone in class with knowledge for their awareness. The reason those types of questions require a new set of skills is because the questions you are now requested to ask changes the paradigm. In Chapter 1, I wrote about a paradigm shift in your thinking. That means you must view your children's knowledge as completely different from what you might have previously believed. Some parents do believe their children are smart—even brilliant—but their children do not see themselves treated as such. Most of the time they are being *"talked at"* instead of *"listened to."* The subtleties of listening and acknowledging what your children know can be misconstrued or taken for granted.

Dialogue is a two-way experience. Research from various authors and educators discuss what happens when we truly listen to someone. Donna Hanak[6] is quoted discussing a learning community for understanding the relationship between parents and children and specified four components, (1) dialogue, (2) listening attentively, (3) elaborating and building on ideas as a contribution to all, and (4) asking

---

[6] Donna Hanak, (2005). *Altering Ways of Being in a Language Arts Classroom*. English Journal, 95(2), 30-34.

each other questions to clarify or expand concepts. Hanak emphasizes the need to engage children in reading material of importance to them. Consequently, teachers must not only ask children what interests them, but *listen* to their answers.

Parents and teachers need to pay attention to their children and try not to make value judgments on what they think their children said. Ask yourself, "What do my children want? How can I instill family values that are important?" Ask them for more details when they share information with you. Also ask your children "how" and "why" questions, not just questions they can answer with a "yes" or "no" response. The process of reflective listening engages you in repeating what you think your child said and asking your child to verify what you heard. As an example, instead of asking your children if they have any homework, ask them what they brought home for homework and have them actually show you. If they have no homework, ask them to show you what they can review.

> **Your words influence how your children think about themselves. Recognize what they know by listening to them so they will be more confident and receptive to accepting themselves.**

How to Harmonize and Find Connections with Your Children

The word *harmonize* is usually related to music and voices singing together. Harmonize (as a metaphor) with your children who have disabilities, especially in the areas of reading, writing, and language arts. Usage of the word harmony began in the Chinese language before the time of Confucius[7]. To be harmonious is to have different viewpoints but understand the relationship of sharing each point of view. When you understand how your children view themselves, and you actively affirm that they have skills and talents, you will find connections with your children.

Finding connections is more than just discussing school-related activities or participating in recreational events. Making connections is also learning from your children. Think of the connections you make

---

[7] The word harmony is pronounced "he" and the Chinese people have a distinct perspective of how it is practiced. They relate harmony to sounds and music but expand on the way it can be interpreted.

19

with your children as a harmony of relations. Harmonizing isn't necessarily agreeing with your children nor having your children agree with you. Open up a dialogue and give them an opportunity to teach you about themselves.

Harmonizing with your children is like a dance that includes sounds of acceptance, acknowledgement, and empowerment.

How to Build Relationships with Your Children—
Becoming Authentic

Building relationships is also part of harmonizing, but the practice of those relationships begins with being authentic. Authenticity is a word that is not used very often to discuss the honesty and integrity of children in relation to their parents. The perception is that a parent is "in charge" of what their children do, so they give directions, hand out consequences for misbehavior, and make decisions on behalf of their children. Building a relationship means that children take an equal part in participating in the decisions made for and about them. The children become active decision makers, which may require compromise from parents and children. That same perception has been true of teachers being in charge in their classrooms. Teachers lead and are usually the final say in a classroom decision. When teachers offer opportunities for children to make classroom decisions, the children "buy in" on what they believe is important to their learning. Additionally, the children want to know that they have some authority over what happens to them in the classroom.

As you begin building a relationship with your children, making a decision to share the authority of decision making in their lives helps them accept more responsibility for the decisions they make. Parents need to know they are not really giving anything up or surrendering authority, rather they are helping their children by accepting what their children offer in the decision-making process. There are many ways parents and teachers can help children by showing their authenticity. Often we do not acknowledge the importance of authenticity as a way of connecting to children. When there is a mutual exchange with children there is also authenticity that children view as having connection and being affirmed.

20

Authenticity is not merely about being honest. You know someone is authentic if he or she is genuine and speaks the truth. When someone is not afraid of saying what's on his or her mind, then deeper trustworthiness can be established. We have a role with children and might not use our authentic selves for fear of giving up the authoritarian role. However, when you tell children you really don't understand something, or tell them your true beliefs, they realize you have human frailties and learn to respond in kind. In other words, your children become authentic. That doesn't mean you are seen as a friend rather than a parent, but they know you make mistakes and have doubts and fears. You then are on equal ground for exchanging communication.

Communication between you and your children needs to be authentic.

Why Passion is the Basis for All We Learn

Passion is the driving force for behavior. Passion is the desire of a tangible object or pleasure that is innate rather than driven by fear. Children who learn what they love are learning through passion. They usually base their concentration and motivation on what they enjoy, which can also be viewed as being passionate. For example, during my graduate school experience my mentor told me about a child she encountered who could not spell simple words, such as *the, had, of,* and *run.* But he could spell the word *horses.* She asked him why he knew how to spell the word horses and he enthusiastically replied, "Because I love them." When children are connected to what they enjoy, they have a more positive attitude toward wanting to learn.

Passion for a subject matter becomes the impetus for learning. Focus on the child instead of the skill development to teach the child to read. It changes the response to the lessons and what is considered important. When teachers and parents focus less on the skills and more on children and what is important to them, it changes the way children behave and the outcome of what they learn or want to learn. I have noticed children's change of behavior and attitude regarding reading when they are asked to share their passions.

Adults engage in activities based on their passions and need to be aware that their children also engage in activities they enjoy. Parents need to accept the notion that children's passions, activities, topics, or things that they enjoy are the foundation for their success in reading, learning to read, and interest in reading. Teachers need to embrace the same paradigm that skills are secondary to concentrating on how learning occurs. The learning process occurs when children are exposed to subjects that peak their interests and are motivated to learn more. Sometimes children focus all their attention on one subject and parents are concerned about them not learning about other subjects. For example, a parent was frustrated when his child was only reading books on horses and felt that his child wasn't getting enough exposure to other subjects. But his child was reading and learning and became interested later in subjects associated with Native American and Spanish cultures related to his learning about horses. As children take new information they learn from one subject, they naturally find other areas of interest. Parents and teachers can guide their children but need to pay attention to what the children enjoy.

How to Tap into Your Child's Passion:
Do You Really Know What Your Child Loves?

Now that you know, you also need to be authentic for communicating effectively with your children, and acknowledge the passions they decide to embrace. Passion is what fuels all of us to act, relate, and participate. As adults we have more choices and many more alternatives to say "yes" or "no" to studying the information we are receiving. However, we don't practice those same principles with our children. If our children say "no," we ask them "why" so many times that they may be inclined to say "yes" just to stop our asking.

We make assumptions about what we know—or think we know—about our children. There are questions we don't ask our children because we assume we can predict their answers. My suggestion for really knowing what your child's passions are is to discuss periodically with them what they like. Don't be afraid to use vocabulary that they may not know. Most children, no matter how young, know what the word *passion* means. Teach them new words like *predilection,* which means bias or affection. Share what your passion was when you were their age. Share something new with your children that they do not know about you. Sometimes we are hesitant to share personal information with our children. But remember, if you are authentic your children may respond positively when you ask them questions.

22

Sharing personal passions can bring you closer to understanding your children.

With your children's interests in mind, it becomes easier to plan activities and events that encourage them to connect these to school subjects. In this way, a child is validated and his or her individuality honored. It may be time consuming to take your children to places to *fuel* their passions. Teachers can tap into your child's passion by giving them an opportunity to share what they know, or by making them a classroom resource for their passion which may be connected to a school subject. Many children are interested in history and are knowledgeable enough to share facts about history with their classmates. When a child, especially one who has a learning disability, has an opportunity to be recognized for something constructive and *shine* in class, he or she needs to be given the chance to be seen in a positive light. There are many circumstances that can help children recognize that their passion matters. Acknowledging your children for their strengths gives them a sense of pride for what they know, which can also fuel their passions. Anything that you can do to help children feel that their passions matter and are contributing to their personal growth, in turn furthering their reading ability, will help them become better readers.

How to Trust in Your Child's Intelligence: Expect More from Your Child Than You Believe They Know

Once you tap into your children's passion and fuel their interests so they can expand their knowledge, you will learn to be more trusting of what your children know. The continued dialogue you have will help you see and recognize their intellectual level. This is of great importance because children with reading problems or learning disabilities have not been able to tap into their own intelligence and continually question their abilities and knowledge. Children who are learning disabled often question the compliments and positive reinforcement given by parents and frequently don't believe them. It appears that children want to have someone other than their parent's compliment or critique them. When an outsider gives them a compliment, it seems more believable. Children who have difficulty in reading may not believe anyone recognizes their talents and skills, which can cause mistrust. Consequently, children will need very specific connections to people who are truthful and more direct with reinforcing comments.

Trusting children to share their knowledge can be as gratifying for the parent as it is for the children. It causes children to know that they matter and that what they know is relevant. Many parents' expectations for their children do not always match what children have as expectations for themselves. You must inform your children about your expectations. When children are part of the decision-making process you get them to trust that you respect their opinion. Parents and teachers make a mistake when they assume they know how intelligent their children are; they don't always know what their children know. Most parents do not tap into the personal knowledge of their children.

Your children really want to be heard. They want to know that you respect their opinion.

When you and your children set expectations together, they accept the standards you set and try to perform at that level. When you "rule" and do not involve them in the decision-making process, they seem to resent doing any of the jobs or activities you impose. If you consider that you are helping your children learn by giving them the responsibility to be involved, you are showing them that you trust in their ability to contribute to their learning. You then acknowledge their intelligence and raise their expectation level for themselves.

How to Have Compassion for Your Child

The word *compassion* is not always used in making a connection with your children. However, I use the word compassion as a reference to strengthen the relationship between you and your children. There are many synonyms that explain compassion and how to interpret what compassion means. *Roget's Thesaurus* uses tolerance, sensitivity, understanding, kindness, and graciousness as synonyms for compassion. When parents or teachers want to give compliments, they may not really know how to state their compliments so they are believable or sincere. There is a fine line between what parents or teachers say and what and how children perceive what they are hearing. There are many circumstances that occur when children misinterpret what is meant to be a compliment. Parents need to think about how children might respond to comments and be more sensitive to their children.

Your children need compassion from you, as well as criticism. Parents need to balance between criticism and praise as learning tools.

How to Emphasize Your Children's Strengths: They Already Know Their Weaknesses

As parents and teachers we try to optimize our children's learning experience. We know about teaching values and providing a great space for them to grow intellectually, emotionally, and spiritually. However, we also assume that it is our responsibility to criticize our children and let them know what they are doing wrong. Simultaneously, we help them correct any behaviors or habits we believe are detrimental to them. As we work with our children, sometimes we are too focused on correcting them and making certain they know what they are doing wrong. Too often we do not spend as much time telling them how proud we are of their positive behavior and their accomplishments. Consequently, children begin to question themselves and believe they are not worthy or can't do anything right. They may get frustrated wanting to please their parents or teachers, but when they continuously hear what they interpret as criticisms, they lose their inner strength for knowing they can be successful. It takes a very observant parent or teacher to balance the criticisms with positive statements. We have a tendency to emphasize the criticisms, not realizing that negative reinforcement is not motivating.

Emphasizing the strengths of our children is more important than pointing out their weaknesses. It is essential to begin an honest dialogue with your children. We sometimes fall short of getting to know our children because we believe we *already* know our children and don't give them the opportunity to share themselves as *they* see themselves.

If you remember that your children need to have both their strengths *and* weaknesses recognized, they may respond more positively. Parenting is a very difficult job that involves a constant stream of messages, and children really want their messages to be positive.

25

Your children may be more likely to share their successes if you ask them what makes them proud.

How to Look for Changes in Your Children

Parents and teachers need to identify changes in their children. There are many clues given to identify these changes. When children become either more excited after attending school or more withdrawn, there are usually reasons for these changes. Often children change their behavior based on how they are treated. Children who are treated as if they are not going to achieve have a mindset that focuses on failure. We have a great deal of influence on our children. When children believe they are not able to succeed, but have been given positive feedback by others, they are able to change their mindset and become successful. How we talk to children really makes a difference in how they see themselves, believe in themselves, and strive to be who they really are. This conversation should also motivate them to gain the strength for self-reliance.

As a parent, teacher, or mentor we set the stage for children's academic and emotional development. We want children to be adaptable and not stagnant, as they may face many obstacles throughout their lives. The world is changing, and adults and children need the ability to cope and adapt to those changes. We can give children a sense of pride by recognizing the positive changes and guiding them with decisions that help them focus on who they really are.

The only constant is change. Realize that your children will change and you *must* prepare them for positive change.

Oftentimes decisions that we make will determine the ability of our children to be effective decision makers. When we focus on leading by example, children have a road map to help them. When children see confidence exhibited by their parents or other adults whom they trust, they learn to emulate that behavior and grow to their ultimate potential. Those decisions also help us see how our children change their behaviors and learn to trust themselves.

Lessons Learned

- Children are effective communicators when they are eager to share their passions. Help them share as part of their reading exercises.
- Sometimes we must change how we treat our children—especially those with disabilities. We cannot assume their capabilities. They are often more capable than we can imagine.
- All children—especially ones with disabilities—need to know they are recognized and empowered. Family members, including the child's siblings, can participate in the child's empowerment.
- Adults need to enable their children to know that everyone, even parents and teachers, make mistakes, have errors which need to be corrected, and have shortcomings or weaknesses.
- When you share personal information with your child, the bond between you becomes stronger.
- Asking your children to help you make decisions will make a difference in how your children treat you. They want to be asked; it adds to their belief that you really truly care about them and respect their intelligence. When you include them, they learn that they make a difference in your life.
- Children usually get more criticism than compassion and those with special education needs really need more compassion than criticism. Compassion comes from an awareness that your children can strive for what you believe they can achieve.
- It doesn't matter whether their success is academic or social; they *want* to be asked for their opinion. They want parents and teachers to recognize their strengths and acknowledge them.
- We need to model what we want our children to do. They watch carefully, and we need to make sure we strive to be good examples.

Summary

Parents and teachers will be amazed at how much their children know and what affect their children's passions have on the improvement of reading. When parents and teachers take an active listening role with their children and are authentically interested in what they know, their children *will* truly amaze them. There are stages in our lives that present different perspectives, and the most important aspect in my experience has been the trust and respect that I give to children. Instead of thinking about the children I teach as "empty" before they come into my class so I can "fill them up with knowledge," I now know that they come to school full of personal knowledge, experience, and passion that can help them learn, share, and transform.

Chapter 3

Why Your Children's Personal Knowledge
is Important to Reading

Shaun was a sixth grader in my colleague's special education classroom. Very frustrated because he was reading at the first-grade level, he still had aspirations of success; he just didn't know how to become a better reader. He came to me very attentive and interested; actually more interested than other children as to how I was going to teach him to read at grade level. What amazed me was Shaun's ability to be interested in so many different topics. He couldn't wait to share all the stories he planned to write. My initial approach was to suggest only six of twelve topics which Shaun would base his stories on for use as his reading text. However, Shaun couldn't wait to share all his passions. In fact he was so happy to talk with me, he announced one day he would be a writer for the world. A child who could barely read knew he had so much to say. I was fascinated. He couldn't wait to get started on writing his first story. He learned so quickly and really liked using the thesaurus to find more descriptive words for his stories. I was delighted that Shaun was so creative and he was excited that I recognized his creativity. After he completed the program and was finally reading at grade level, I asked him to write a testimonial for my file. He wrote, "I have learned phenomenal amounts in this program. I use my affirmation, 'I am trusting myself with the right answer. Now I know I can use my independence to become a writer for the world.' It's hard to realize now, that I went from first-to-sixth-grade reading in just a dozen study sessions."

Shaun taught me how valuable a child's personal knowledge is to reading. As children learn that they have knowledge and understanding of their favorite activities, or special time they may spend with family, friends, and other passions, they build upon those experiences to help learn or improve their reading skills. As adults we have more choices to decide what we prefer and how to use those choices to gain information; choices which lead us to be good decision makers. We need to offer our children the same opportunities. As Shaun says, *"I am trusting myself with the right answers."* Teaching our children that their knowledge is the basis for decisions that they make—and that those decisions shape how they feel about themselves—can send messages that they are either worthy or unworthy.

Knowledge and opinions matter, and parents and teachers should be encouraged to acknowledge children's viewpoints. As children acquire knowledge, they need to be recognized for that and know that knowledge originating from their personal experiences can help them improve their reading skills. When children read about what they know, it gives them confidence that they can achieve more.

Personal knowledge is an important foundation to help children learn to improve their reading.

Why Reading is Already Within the Child

Since it is determined that children come to school with a 25,000-word vocabulary before they are four years of age, children have the capacity to use their language as the basis for reading. The most important aspect of their vocabulary is children's understanding of these words and their thoughts about what they are learning intuitively. As they grow, intellectually they are comprehending information from the vocabulary and concepts to which they are exposed. When children learn new words, they are also learning how these new words represent meaning. For example, even at the age of two or three a child knows the difference between a mouse that is a rodent and a mouse that is an accessory to the computer. At a very young age children know the subtleties of language. Parents and teachers need to be aware that children are like sponges and absorb so much more than we think they can. When children are exposed to new words and can express their own thoughts using those words, their new knowledge is the foundation for reading and comprehending.

Reading begins with the child's language. Oral language is the foundation for understanding, a key factor in reading success.

Children need to be taught that their knowledge related to their interest can contribute to what Dr. Paulo Freire notes as *"reading the world."* When children are exposed to subjects of their interest, they have all the possibilities of potential for reading the world. Specifically, exposure to any subject through observation, listening, dialogue, and sharing what a person knows is the basis for reading. Children read the world every day. They use learned information to decipher new, and as

30

yet unfamiliar, information. Learning language and how to speak at ages of up to four years is not a skill that parents teach. Children that have all their senses pay attention to their surroundings and watch everything they touch. Remember, infants typically put everything they can touch into their mouths. That is their way of learning how something feels.

Developmentally, children learn in stages. Jean Piaget used his own children to write books about how children develop and learn. He observed his two children every day and noted *everything* they did. He created the various cognitive learning stages of children from infants to 11 years and older. From birth to age two, the first stage, a child uses 100 percent of his or her sensory motor skills for learning and developing cognitively. From two to seven years, the preoperational stage, children learn language by using words and pictures and express themselves through these objects. They believe the world revolves around them. Children from age seven to 11 are beginning to understand concepts and different points of view and can order objects by size, color, and shape. They comprehend the converse of numbers; if 4 + 3 = 7, then 7 - 4 = 3. This is the concrete operational stage; they can reason that the same amount of liquid can be held in a tall thin cup as well as a short wide cup. Children's thinking is still at this concrete stage whereby they need to *see* everything. Children's reasoning is still from a comparison of what they see. The last stage of Piaget's developmental model is from 11 years and beyond. This stage, formal operational, revolves around children's abilities to think abstractly. Children reason and debate based on information they have gathered from their life experiences, which involve learning how to argue, prove a point, and analyze. This stage becomes a foundation for children's logical reasoning and a strong desire to "come into their own."

Parents are their children's first teachers. As parents learn about the stages of their children's development, they need to be aware that not every child moves through the stages chronologically.

Why Vocabulary Increases Comprehension

As parents learn they are the first and actually the best teachers for their children, they are also the first people in their children's life to hear them speak. We don't teach our children to speak, but we encourage their speech and listen to how they learn to pronounce words. A parent reflects on the first words their children learn, possibly mispronouncing a word that becomes a comical experience for everyone and an embarrassing experience for the children. Therefore, as they are speaking new words that they have heard from others, they are also comprehending what the words mean. There is a natural progression of how children learn to speak in a sentence. No one teaches young children between one and two years how to talk in sentences. First they learn whole words; usually a child's first word is *"mommy."* Then they say *"mommy go."* Very soon after that, as children add words to their vocabulary, they form those words into a sentence or question, so "mommy go" becomes "Mommy, can we go?" Children learn through imitation and repetition. Meanings of vocabulary are incorporated into their learning process. Children intuitively understand meanings because they sense emotion and use other senses to know what words mean.

For example, when I was reading with a child with a severe learning disability and wrote the affirmation *I am brilliant* for the child to repeat, the child read the sentence but with very little emotion or feeling. When I asked the sentence to be read with **conviction**, he sat straight up in his chair and read loudly I AM BRILLIANT. I had not taught him the meaning of the word conviction and had never used it in his presence, but he knew exactly what I meant. I knew at that very moment that children know more than we give them credit for. I knew then that their oral vocabulary would be an asset to their ability to read or learn to read. The practical ways children learn are related to research, but parents and teachers need to be aware that their ability to share language with their children will be a vital piece of improving children's reading levels. Remember, as a parent you are your child's first teacher.

Vocabulary increases every day because young children are exposed to so many words. They use these words in their daily lives and practice them in sentences. Children hear inflections and imitate what they hear. Even deaf children can *hear* their mother's voice through touch, sight, smell, and vibration. As children observe their environment, they learn new words and learn to understand their surroundings. Children practice object comparisons, like Piaget's example of learning that every animal they see is not a cat, but once they identify a dog, the children can now make comparisons of animals. Using these examples, the ability to comprehend information is integrated into learning and using vocabulary words. The most significant difference is that children are not specifically taught these words. They learn them through use and exposure. That is the reason vocabulary increases children's comprehension. Children develop those processes *before* they ever enter school.

How to Talk to Your Children and
Build Their Reading Language

Once parents realize the value and long-term effects of how and why vocabulary builds children's comprehension, they need to take an active role in helping their children build comprehension skills. Research has found that parents who speak to their children articulating words correctly will help their children with pronunciation. The correct pronunciation of words results in the children's accuracy of pronunciation and learning the comprehension of vocabulary. Conversing with your child is an important step in their language development and prepares them for reading successfully.

Speak to your children using adult language, not baby talk. Use a vocabulary which prepares them to converse effectively.

Continuing the dialogue as your children are in school is extremely important. Many parents ask questions when their children come home from school, but are answered with short responses or most times with one-word responses. Questions like, "How was your day in school?" or "What did you learn in school today?" Children typically answer with responses such as "fine" or "same old thing." The problem is that parents need to concentrate on questions where children need to explain their answers or elaborate on talking about something from their school day. The questions from parents need to be very specific and directly related to the topic or subject matter that they are learning in school. A more involved question to ask your child is, "What did the teacher tell you about the missions that you are studying? What was the most important thing you learned that you didn't know? How do you think the missions would survive today?" The questions also need to be age and subject matter appropriate. Usually in first grade children learn about people that help us, for example, policemen, firemen, doctors, and nurses. Parents need to ask questions about their child's individual knowledge regarding the people who help others. The most important point in talking to your children is to have an open dialogue every day. You must also consider what they are interested in discussing. Be aware if they don't want to discuss some subjects. Be mindful that they may be hesitant for a reason. Take note of their responses and continue open dialogue.

Language is not a skill that people teach. Every child learns language in the same way. What happens to children as they mature is a reinforced set of verbal cues that are found through imitation. But language is very valuable as a communication skill. It helps our ability to write and to share our writing. Children need to learn that writing and reading are based on learning that language skills are the impetus for writing and reading. Once you build a child's language vocabulary you automatically build speaking and writing vocabulary. Using *Roget's Thesaurus* also builds children's vocabulary.

Find ways to challenge your children's vocabulary. Have them conduct their own research and acknowledge different words to say that enhance what they write. Although many parents or single parents hold two jobs and have very little time to spend with their children, it is important to note that talking to children can increase their vocabulary. Parents can arrange a "message board" where children write notes to their parent(s). A tidbit, a joke, or something that the child is passionate about can help gain skills in reading and writing. Parents can institute the message board as a communication between their children and themselves. This practice of using the message board may give children the connection they are missing when parents can't spend the time. Be creative and think of other ways parents can reinforce their children's verbal language development.

Advice and Actions to Empower Your Children to Read

The emphasis in this chapter is on parents reinforcing their children's vocabulary to assist them with reading and comprehension. Specific advice and actions begin with parents' and teachers' acknowledgment of children learning new words. A thesaurus, rather than a dictionary, is a better reference book for synonyms and reinforcing children's language development. However, the dictionary as a resource book does have a place in the child's learning. Dictionaries help with word origin, pronunciation, meaning, and sometimes provide a sentence so the child reads the word in context. A thesaurus is a quick way to increase the vocabulary for children. I have found that children enjoy the sound of words and they have an interest and enthusiasm for learning new words.

Advice 1: Have your child choose a new word and *highlight that word on his/her bedroom wall.* This can be done using chart paper or setting up a whiteboard. Then have the child write a sentence on the message board highlighting the new word. That sentence can also be their affirmation of the day or week (explained later in this chapter).

Advice 2: A new word should be chosen every day and one word during the week can be highlighted to use in the child's conversation.

Advice 3: If your child is a reluctant reader, have him choose a favorite story and find a time to read. Read a page and have your child read a page. That way your child sees and hears you reading and you have set an example that reading is a pleasurable experience.

Advice 4: After your child has chosen a book, ask him or her to predict the story by looking at the book jacket. Even before your child begins reading, he or she will have a focus. When a child has focus reading becomes purposeful. Predicting the story also gives the child focus to find out if the prediction was correct, close to being correct, or completely wrong. New vocabulary is also generated with predictions. Since predicting story outcomes is related to reading comprehension, it is advantageous to help your child anticipate the story content. Always accept the child's prediction because even if it's not logical you are still helping your child with the thinking skills needed to understand what is being read.

Advice 5: Find time once a week for the family—*everyone* in the family—to read together. Choose an area in the home and call it the "book nook" or "reading corner." Set it up as a space and make it a designated reading area. Have chairs or bean bag seating so the area has a feeling of warmth and comfort. With a special time and place, you show your child, who is a reluctant or frustrated reader, that reading is important and that reading can be an activity for the whole family. Your children can bring anything to read to this space; reading something that peaks their interest will help them know they can be successful readers. Be sure to tell them words they can't pronounce rather than have them guessing at words they don't know. Any information you can give your children so they are not frustrated is important.

Action 1: Getting your children to enjoy reading means providing books related to their passion. It's okay for them to read every book about horses. Let them become experts.

Action 2: As a parent or teacher you can help children be confident about their reading by assigning them as "resource experts" for a subject in the classroom or at home. Many children love all kinds of animals and they need to be recognized for their expertise. Arrange a trip to the zoo and tell the child who is a reluctant reader that he or she will be an expert for the day. Then set up questions for the children and have your reluctant reader be the expert to answer the classroom questions. For example, a question could be to explain the difference between orangutans and chimpanzees, which can be answered after the children see the animals.

Action 3: Reluctant readers also like to help others. Enable your child to be a mentor for a younger child. Depending on their current reading level, if they are able to read first-grade books or picture books with very few words, have them read to a child in kindergarten or first grade.

Action 4: Encourage children to read as often as you can. Children respond more positively to encouragement than to criticism. Encourage them to be verbal about what they know as they read their stories. Encouragement is also the prerequisite to empowerment. Children need to know that people appreciate what they know.

> **These advice and action tips need to be focused on positive encouragement resulting in empowering children and reinforcing the importance of reading.**

Empowering your children helps them realize their potential and capabilities. The advice and actions are brief practices that help suggest and reinforce how to acknowledge children who need extra support for self-empowerment. When children have difficulty reading, you spend time paying close attention to what they know and less attention on teaching skill development. If these children were able to learn through skill development, they wouldn't have difficulty reading or need a paradigm shift to learn and improve their reading skills.

Why Parents and Teachers Need to Introduce Affirmations

An affirmation is a positive statement about anything. It is important to introduce affirmations to children with learning disabilities. I tell children "an affirmation is a positive statement about you." The reason I introduce affirmations as a part of the **You Read** structure is to enable children to truly *believe* in themselves and know that they can learn to read, improve their reading skills, and understand that their *potential is unlimited.*

I remember a ninth-grade student who became emotional during his first hour with me. I was puzzled, so I asked him what was wrong. He said very emphatically, "Dr. Stone these are *not* tears of sorrow, these are tears of joy. I know now I can finally learn to read!" This was a new belief he discovered; that he could believe he was smart and had the ability to learn to read. He just needed a different approach to learn.

Introducing affirmations gives children a sense that they can accomplish anything. It gives them the reassurance that they *can* truly learn to read sufficiently and be independent readers. Affirmations also help children focus on their strengths. Since all affirmations begin with an *I am* statement meaning selfishness, it is important to stress to children that *I am* is not selfish, but rather an emphasis on who they *really* are and who they can *become* after they have learned to read.

Affirmations are statements children learn and repeat because they need to be reminded that they are important. If we remember what students really need emotionally, we should incorporate affirmations in their daily lessons and integrate positive feelings about themselves.

Incorporate affirmations in every child's life. They will feel the strength of their own resolve. "I am a powerful reader" is a great place to start.

An important lesson during the sessions of **You Read** is that children's intuition helps them achieve at their highest level. "I am a stupendous learner" is another affirmation most children accept. My most memorable affirmation was from Shaun, who questioned his decisions about answers on his work or tests he had to take. We decided together that he *knew* what the answers were and he needed to make sure that he didn't question his decisions. Shaun needed an affirmation to match what he truly believed about himself. We wrote, "I am trusting myself with the right answer" as an affirmation for his sense of knowing. He continued to choose affirmations that related to what he knew he could accomplish as he approached his academic tasks, especially those related to reading. Children know more than adults credit them. They can sense what is right for them, but many times teachers and parents don't seem to get the messages. The essence of children to affirm themselves or what they are doing is of great significance. The fact they already know or have a sense of knowing reinforces their intuitive understanding. Affirmations are a way these children recognize their own strengths and sustain their knowledge.

How to Help Your Children Practice Affirmations

Now that I have explained what affirmations are and the importance of children reciting affirmations, I want to reinforce the way parents and teachers can promote their use of affirmations. Make certain the first affirmation you write is very directed to what your child needs to know about himself. It should be based on what your child is struggling with, but always using *I am* statements to empower the child. It might be advantageous to include other children in the family so every child has a separate specific affirmation. Set up a time for the children to repeat their affirmations to you and to their siblings. Affirmations are scheduled several times a day so that children are sure to have reinforcement. When I ask children to practice affirmations, I tell them they can read or recite them in the mirror, to any family member, or even a pet. The most valuable and essential lesson concerning affirmations is that children really take time to believe what they are saying about themselves and practice what the affirmation means. If they say they are trusting themselves with the right answer, they need to really practice self-trust. If they say they are powerful readers, they need to believe the skills they are learning are helping them read independently. The affirmations are not just static phrases, but truly positive thoughts about how children perceive themselves.

Affirmations are statements that can assist children in the process of developing or supporting a positive self-image. Children with learning disabilities tend to have very low self-esteem. After many years of helping these children believe they have the capacity and capability of becoming proficient readers, I know that it takes time and energy, and the belief of others to give them the confidence to be successful readers. Those who come in contact with children who have reading difficulties need to make sure they are positive role models. There are many reasons that children need affirmations and providing them with positive statements concerning their self-worth will give them a feeling of success, even if they have not fully experienced the success in reading they desire. Affirmations enable children with difficulties to change their thinking so that they can see how success feels. I want to stress that anyone who works with children, especially children with disabilities, needs to recognize one of the goals of education is to acknowledge their strengths.

How children feel about themselves is directly connected to their achievement in all areas of their lives.

There has been too much emphasis on children's weaknesses related to their learning disabilities. There needs to be a balance between emphasizing children's strengths verses weaknesses. When children with disabilities try to compete with their peers in the classroom, they experience negativity based upon what they observe regarding the speed and agility of the academic level of children without any apparent disability. Teachers emphasize the fact that everyone has strengths and weaknesses, but those who teach children with disabilities more often concentrate on their weaknesses. Changes need to happen in the teaching of reading in order to promote the success of the children with disabilities. Parents and teachers can take an innovative view of their children and help them progress not only academically but also emotionally, strengthening their self-esteem.

 **Lessons Learned**

- Consider your children having equal or more knowledge of a subject matter than what you expect. Children need to be credited for their knowledge.

- Speak intelligently to your children and teach them to emphasize their new vocabulary.

- Rely on parental instincts to prepare your child for "reading the world." Help your children develop intellectually, remembering Piaget's cognitive stages.

- The more language you use to teach your children, the more they hear and understand. That means language and vocabulary are definitely connected to help children specifically understand conversations.

- The advice and actions will help parents focus on praising their children. Children do not really want to be disruptive; they want to be accepted in spite of the difficulties they encounter.

- Children with disabilities need to feel empowered and affirmations help them see and believe they have the aptitude, capability, and talent to be accomplished readers.

- When teachers and parents stress the importance of affirmations, children can learn to practice affirmations. Affirmations help children become more motivated and focused on what they need to learn.

Summary

You Read focuses on children's personal knowledge as a foundation for developing reading skills. Since children's knowledge is at the forefront of the program, it frames each session and contributes to each child's successful reading experience. Children spend significant time with mentors. These are examples in which a parent can talk to their children as a process of engaging children in speaking about themselves and learning how to *really* connect in a conversation. Learning what children care about, as they increase their vocabulary and express their interests are basic factors to learning to read and improving reading skills. Parents and teachers need to adapt to *and* adopt a new system, and understand that children's ideas are the brick and mortar of their ability to improve their reading skills. Vocabulary building and understanding the meaning of words is a cornerstone of **You Read**. Children need the introduction of age-appropriate words in spite of their difficulty with reading. Children like the sound of words and learn from words they like to hear. The Advice and Actions presented in this chapter need to be used often.

Another emphasis in this chapter is learning and practicing affirmations. A very important aspect of **You Read** is affirmations. We all need to incorporate affirmations in daily reading sessions. However, it is also important to emphasize to children that the affirmations chosen are authentic and have real meaning for each child. Affirmations are to be used as reinforcement to help children know how *positive statements* can change the way they view themselves. An affirmation every day that children read, remember, and are proud to say aloud will increase their self-confidence.

Chapter 4

Skill Development Begins with the Child— *Not* the Reading Skills

*Drew was entering the first grade when her dad brought her to me for reading instruction. Her mother was not sure the program would help, but agreed to have her try. Her father spoke about his problem as a child with dyslexia and wanted his daughter to receive the help he didn't get as a child. Drew had bright eyes and a winning smile. As a six-year-old with virtually no reading skills, she was eager to learn. She did have dyslexia, and as she took my assessment baseline grade level, she was unable to pass the first-grade passage. So I didn't frustrate her by asking her to read further. When we started the **You Read** program, and she gave me topics that were of interest, her eyes lit up as she became excited about sharing her ability to draw and ride her bike. I wanted to have her dictate five sentences, but felt she could only read three sentences back to me. However, the more I wrote the more she wanted me to write. As our sessions progressed, Drew was learning and retaining her stories. Comprehension was very easy for her. She showed creativity and had the oral vocabulary to add many adjectives to her stories.*

*I talked recently with Drew who is now fourteen. Although her mother was skeptical of the program working at first, she is very proud of her. Drew shared that during her eighth-grade year she received all A's and B's with an A+ in English language arts. I asked her if she were interested in becoming a writer. She said she loved children and her goal was to study medicine and become a pediatric oncologist. In retrospect, she was so happy she had the **You Read** experience because her favorite activity was reading. She loved to read everything.*

This chapter should really be titled "Talk is *Not* Cheap, It Teaches Children to Read." **You Read** is a copyrighted program and its theories are based on holistic principles. That means that skill development is weaved in the children's stories. Skills are taught as an integral part of story development and part of the whole process. The most powerful aspect of the program is that all skill development is based on stories that each child dictates to me or a reading instructor. After each story, comprehension questions follow. These questions are authentic and asked by mentors to tap into what the children think and believe to be most effective answers. I am confident after using **You Read** that children's propensity for their answers originates from their personal knowledge of the subject for which they are familiar.

Skill development is individualistic. As a teacher or parent you can't depend on skills to be the primary source of learning or improving reading.

As each child answers the mentor's questions, there is a confidence that is established so that each child feels he or she has mastered the reading process. Since **You Read** is structured entirely with the child in mind, the skills become an essential and connected part of the process. Skills, in fact, are part of the *hole* which is missing in learning to read, but are taught as a *whole* in the structure of teaching reading.

Grade-Level Standards and Fallacies
for Children in Special Education

Education Week [8] and the Institute of Education Science reported that the United States government spent over $1 billion dollars in 2014 for Reading First, a federally funded program for states to assist children in kindergarten through third grade in reading skills, so every child can read at grade level by third grade. A Reading First committee was established to determine how the Reading First grant will assist the United States Government's No Child Left Behind law, to improve academic skills for all children. Since the No Child Left Behind law was enacted in 2002, there has been very little impact, if any, for increasing children's reading levels and ability for stronger comprehension skills. This funding was for children *without* disabilities and the results have shown no improvement in literacy scores or rates of growth in reading. Because of the lack of reading improvement, governors and education commissioners revamped the requirements to improve children's level of literacy through a common core of reading skills. State committees have individually instituted a Common Core of new approaches with the emphasis on vocabulary building. Reading First is still developing the structure of how the Common Core is going to assist children who are not literate or reading at-or-above grade level. The additional emphasis is on the content of the reading material. However, when children haven't been exposed to the content and expected to comprehend, they will still have difficulty. The reports present changes,

---

[8] *Education Week*, November 12, 2014.

but if we contrast these changes with the high percentage of children and adults who are below grade level in reading or functionally illiterate, we are still not achieving the goal of grade-level reading proficiency for all children. The report also stresses that children in middle school and high school can read, but don't comprehend the material they are reading. The children have become "word callers." The purpose of the critique is to *change* the current paradigm on which the committee has based its restructuring of the reading curriculum. Educators have admitted they have not been cognizant of what must change in the United States for its children to increase their reading strengths and levels.

My research and experience have indicated that it is fine to create and develop new procedures, programs, and approaches to help raise the literacy rates of school-age children, but if we are using the same philosophy about how children learn, and what we as reading teachers must do to help children improve, the new programs, procedures, and curricula will fall short of making the expected gains we are hoping to achieve. The basis for change is the need to look at how we *believe* children learn. I have said that parents do not teach their children to talk. Even researchers studying second-language learners or foreign-born children acknowledge that children learn to speak their native language through imitation of their parents. Children listen, observe, and respond in kind. Reading instruction should be direct and child centered and the core standards should begin with the philosophy of how children learn.

We must consider paying closer attention to the paradigm that learning occurs within children as they react and respond to their environment, people, and activities. Jean Piaget, after watching his own children grow and learn, noted that their development was based on how they played, reacted to people, and developed language. He structured his processes into a series of stages that educators still use today to explain children's mental and physical development. Although we still use Piaget's seminal research to model and watch our children's growth, there are definite changes in our world. With constant evolving technology, young children have become smarter and proficient in the educational learning community. As a result of these changes we also need to change our educational philosophy and adopt new practices, such as using the constructivist approach to deliver quality instruction. Constructivist teaching begins with a foundation that children construct their own meaning of material they read. They are active not passive learners, contributing their own knowledge to subject matter.

We must review the philosophy we have used in the past in order to change the results. Accepting a new philosophy and rearranging how we deliver instruction is the foundation for the new programs. The underlying foundation helps bring about change.

Misconceptions regarding standards are that children in special education classes are able to fulfill the general education grade-level norms. While the U.S. Department of Education is developing grade-level standards, it does not consider children with special needs and assumes that those standards apply to *all* children. However, because of various limitations and varying degrees of learning differences children in special education have, they are *not* able to reach standards. There should be a measurement of their abilities. For example, one of the standards in reading and language arts for a fifth-grade student is the requirement of using figurative language. Children with special education needs do not usually have an understanding of figurative language. If you ask a child designated to have special education needs what it means when people say, *"It's raining cats and dogs,"* the child will tell you cats and dogs are falling from the sky. Standardization needs to be restructured and children in special education need to be taught about figurative language. Any number of those types of standards, regardless of grade level, cannot be applied to children receiving special education services. Instead of transferring general education standards as a requirement for children in special education placements, the standards need to be rewritten for practical and doable achievement that children in a special educational setting can attain.

When skills are emphasized first, children with a special education diagnosis have difficulty in mastering the skill levels. When children are tested and diagnosed with learning disabilities, the federal law requires them to receive a specific individual education plan (IEP), *individualized* for them. Every child's IEP is a set of standards written by a committee that includes parents, teachers, administrators, and oftentimes the children themselves. One important aspect of the IEP meeting is to look at a standardization of the child's capabilities and write goals that match those expectations. This cannot be accomplished by using general education grade-level standards. All goals and objectives geared toward children's instruction are written down and signed by all parties who participate. These standards are based on what the committee believes will help a child achieve these goals. Standardization is based on a set of criteria that directly relates to the needs of the children with disabilities. Whether the children have learning or more severe disabilities, the standards are very specific because each standard is based on their IEP achievable goals.

Public Law 94-142 Changed Educating Children with Handicapping Conditions

The general education standards are based on an educator's perspective of what children need for a particular grade level. However, those standards can be arbitrary depending upon the educator's departmental office and their beliefs and philosophy regarding learning, obtaining information, and knowledge children should have. Standards for children with disabilities need to be specifically designed to meet individual needs. In 1975, *PL94-142 Education for All Handicapped Children Act* was created specifically to address the academic and behavioral difficulties of children with disabilities. Before 1975, children with disabilities were not required to attend public schools. In fact, as research data reports, many children whose parents requested school attendance were rejected because the schools did not have adequate placements or facilities to teach them. Teachers were not trained to teach children with disabilities. Parents were told their children should stay home. If parents couldn't care for their children, many of these children were placed in institutions for the handicapped. The times were very bleak for any child with a handicapping condition to progress and receive appropriate education for their needs.

Before 1975, standards for children with handicapping conditions were very low and children did not receive any public services toward an education. These children were not given any opportunities for progressing, especially in an academic setting. All their needs were cared for either in their homes or in institutions. School districts were within their legal right to refuse school attendance for children with disabilities.

46

It took several decades for parents to come together to protest the accepted system in place and change the conditions so their children would receive a public education. The changes for educational services initially occurred state by state. Wisconsin and Massachusetts were trend-setters in protesting schools' refusal to educate children with handicapping conditions. Parents lobbied throughout the country, state by state, to protest schools' insistence that their handicapped or disabled children couldn't attend school. Parents were instrumental in the passage of each state law to educate their children in school. State representatives were driven and determined to help parents realize their efforts to establish a national law requiring all school districts throughout the country to educate their children with special needs.

The creation of PL94-142 took many years to develop before becoming law. Attitudes and practices of public schools began to change in the field of education throughout the country. University teacher education departments developed programs to train teachers for their new role teaching children with disabilities. Courses in diagnostic procedures and curricula development, specifically designed to help children with disabilities develop their intellectual potential and social emotional growth, were seen as advancing the educational constructs for children with disabilities. There was now definite progress in educating children with disabilities.

Several factors were included as part of the law to help determine how children were identified and educated so that they would receive an education equal to that of their non-handicapped peers. First, children who had disabilities were to be identified in each school across the country by a provision called Child Find. Second, children were to be evaluated by a school psychologist so they would be properly educated. Parents were included in the evaluation process. Third, a meeting was held so that an IEP was created to assist students, teachers, parents, and anyone else designated to work with the child. This plan was mandated for each child educated under the PL94-142. The IEP designation ensured that all children could be given the opportunity to succeed at their own level and at their own pace. Fourth, children with handicapping conditions were to be educated in the Least Restrictive Environment (LRE), an appropriate placement that didn't separate the children from their peers. Fifth, parents had a right to due process for their children. If parents thought the school was not doing its due diligence to educate their children, they could take the school district to court to change the way their child was educated. The most important point was that children with handicapping conditions were now required—by law—to be educated with their peers. Parents had rights to demand their child's appropriate and free public education.

Education is a right for all children. Children with handicapping conditions deserve the opportunity to have a free public education.

In 2004, PL94-142 was updated and became known as Individuals with Disabilities Education Act (IDEA). The changes that were made involved incorporating children with handicapping conditions into the organization of Americans with Disabilities. This was suggested and mandated so that children would also have the same rights as adults with handicapping conditions. Parents wanted to have their children protected under a law that would be applicable for life. The children included in the law would have all the equal opportunities, reasonable accommodations, and due process available to every person with a disability.

The *difference* between PL94-142 and IDEA is that any child diagnosed with a disability and receiving special education services in school can *now* continue to receive services after they graduate from school, as long as they have been classified with a handicapping condition. Under IDEA, after age 22, they can receive all the services persons with a handicapping condition receive throughout their lifetime.

Educational Core Standards of Children with Disabilities

Public Law 94-142 developed standards that are structured for various disabilities of children educated in the public schools. When the law was created, parents and legislators knew that children with disabilities would have a difficult time adhering to regular educational standards for general education students. Therefore, educational standards needed revision and the current law representing children with special needs, IDEA 2004, had revisions incorporated into the American with Disabilities (ADA) law. These revisions have added the categorical definition and handicapping condition of autism, ADD, and ADHD to the classification for children and reinforced the current classification of dyslexia. The educational standards are significantly different because they are written individually for each child with special needs, and the law has designated these educational standards as an IEP for each child diagnosed under the special education IDEA law revised in 2004.

Special education teachers use a child's IEP as the standardization for the child's success. Children are not only taught to fulfill each goal, but as they progress through their original goals, they are presented with new goals that fulfill the education standards specific to their needs. Sometimes it takes a child several years to achieve one specific goal, depending on the severity of the child's disability. The goals are carried over each year and the child spends time with a special education teacher. All time devoted to helping children with their goals is documented. Throughout the year, each child is tested and the results of each test are used to determine the child's progress.

Since children in special education programs are working at their own pace, it is important to acknowledge the child for the progress made. Children in special education placements have specific standards. Educational standards are created through the objectives, goals, and progress of the child's IEP. Reporting on each child's academic or behavior improvement is based on the specific goals and objectives written from the IEP. The child's standards are based on collaboration of members of the IEP committee and what the law specifies as appropriate skills related to capabilities for children diagnosed with a particular disability. Therefore, standardization is targeted to apply to children who have a similar ability or disability.

Standards for children diagnosed as needing special education services are particular to the abilities and disabilities that those children exhibit.

Standardization is also applied to any special education student who has been, or is included in, regular education classes. As the law is interpreted from school districts, it promotes a system known as inclusion or mainstreaming. According to Albert Shanker of the American Federation of Teachers, standards need to be adapted for all learning styles that children exhibit. However, the law doesn't *require* general standards to be rewritten. It is *only* a suggestion. The IEP was devised for differentiated classroom instruction mandated by public law.

Regrettably, school districts are still holding children with special education needs accountable for general education standards. It is confusing for both the teachers and children who have an IEP in place. The educators writing the general education standards and those writing the special education standards need to collaborate on the most effective means for assuring that children with special education needs meet viable standards for *their* academic improvement.

Education standards applicable to all teachers, whether they are general or special education teachers, are in need of being revised to fulfill the tenet of differentiated standards. This means that teachers can address a variety of learning styles and abilities. When teachers use a process of brainstorming for ideas of what children want to learn, they are differentiating instruction. Another example is planning assignments with different levels of difficulty. The topic or story is read and learned by all students, but some students would only answer certain comprehension questions. Differentiated instruction helps all children and there is a need for that process to be part of the state and federal government. More thought needs to include differentiated instruction in the core standards.

There is justification to have core standards for teaching children; however, the individuals who create those common core standards often fail to include those who teach special education students and who are cognizant about the needs and differentiated standards that apply to these children. Leaders lead by example, but if they do not have knowledge of how children with special education needs learn, they cannot contribute to the development of standardization for these children.

Assessment measures relating to Common Core standards are also important in children's development, and especially to their abilities. Children need to be assessed at all levels in their development and the primary assessment is in academic curriculum areas, as well as socialization areas. General educators have not been able to understand the unique abilities that children with special needs have, and therefore cannot effectively design assessment tools necessary and adequate for understanding the way in which these children learn.

It is important to include special education teachers in developing assessment tools and a set of core standards for children with special needs.

Assessing Children with Disabilities

Children with disabilities are assessed individually. Since disabilities are specific to each child, progress indicators are also individualized. The law designates that all children referred for special education must be assessed with qualified tools that psychologists and teachers of special education use to diagnose any learning, intellectual, emotional abilities, or disabilities. Assessment results provide teachers and psychologists with applicable information to determine whether children have any learning, intellectual, or emotional disabilities and how to proceed with their educational needs. Children's assessments are mandated by IDEA, but are used to write objectives related to their learning profiles. Therefore, curricula that incorporate children's objectives may not be at grade level. Assessment is the tool that is used to determine how to proceed with children who have special education needs. Improving student learning is not based solely on what a general education curricula provides. It is based on children's specific weaknesses and strengths. Once those specifics are identified, the children's IEP is developed and written. Particular assessments are then given once a year and a total assessment is given every three years, which includes an IQ test as part of the comprehensive group of assessments. There is no shortage of assessments for children with special education needs. The assessments are used so children's academic needs are met from the standardization of helping them achieve at their individual level.

The major difference between the core standards written for children in general education and the standards written for children in special education classes is that *the personalized attention children with special needs receive from their IEP achievable goals* is based on their weaknesses. Most decisions are based on the children's personalization, regardless of the diagnosis. There is a second set of standards for children with special needs, but if they were measured by the core standards, evaluation might not be appropriate for their individual needs. Educators developing core standards need to be cognizant of what is viable for children with special needs.

51

Core standards were created without consideration of children with special needs. Even after children were required to receive a mainstream education, educators have not considered their individual needs.

General Education Class Placement

When children with special education needs are placed in a general education class, it is assumed that they can function similar to children without special needs. The problem is that general education teachers are not trained in techniques and procedures that the federally mandated IDEA requires. The model that has been adopted is the consultant model. Sometimes referred to as co-teaching, the districts have made dyads or a collaboration with two teachers serving students together for the general education classrooms. A special education teacher co-teaches in a subject area in the general education classroom and works with children classified as needing special services. These children are included in the general education classroom so they can remain with their peers, but have the services of a special education teacher. Additionally, the special education instructor teaches other children working below grade level that may not be diagnosed or classified as needing special education services. School districts interpret the law for inclusion of children with special education needs. The problem with total inclusion is the need for some children to receive services from a special education teacher—individually—not in a mainstreaming or inclusive situation. Not all children with special education needs can function in a general education class for an entire day without being seen physically in a separate room. The special education resource teachers should be given an opportunity to decide how certain children receive their services.

When children are placed in a general education classroom, no consideration is given for their IEP. According to IDEA, each child with a special education diagnosis receives an IEP acknowledging strengths and weaknesses. Goals are then written, with parent or guardian approval, for helping the child achieve academically, concentrating on remediating the child's weaknesses. When the IEP goals are not fulfilled, children with special needs may not progress. This lack of fulfillment may result in the school district, classroom

52

teacher, or special education teacher being in noncompliance with the law.

It is very important to include every child diagnosed with a special need in the regular education classroom. However, IDEA also requires school placement in a classroom to be in the Least Restrictive Environment (LRE). When children's special education needs designated by a school committee are too severe for a regular education placement, there needs to be the option for separate classroom placement. At the time of the IEP meeting, the committee can suggest times or locations where the special needs child can be included in general education activities. These activities are based on the child's weaknesses *as well as* strengths.

We must think of all aspects of the child with special education needs, as well as the children in the general education classroom, and how all the children will relate to each other.

Children need to be asked what they want, and their opinion also needs to be considered before making decisions about their inclusion in general education classes. Even if we are discussing the inclusion of a young child who is kindergarten age, we need to know how comfortable that child will feel. Within the school classroom, most often children are not asked what they think or how they will feel.

Children with special education needs have an opinion and an idea of what's best for them. Even children who are non-verbal have a way of communicating their needs.

The success of children included in a general education classroom depends on many factors. The first consideration is whether those children are going to feel comfortable surrounded by their peers and how they believe they can contribute to the general education class. The next consideration is their ability to be a part of the group of children in spite of their disabilities. When a decision is made to include them, but their opinion is not solicited, it sends a message that their opinion isn't valued in the general education classroom. A high percentage of children included in a general education class do very well with the additional assistance from a special education teacher. Many district practices do not offer outside classroom help where students can go to a separate location with the special education teacher to complete work or receive extra help. Since school districts have adopted the co-teaching process where general education and special education are taught in the same room, the system doesn't provide outside-class help.

It would be advantageous to offer co-teaching opportunities as well as outside help. There has been motivation for change and encouragement to provide more general education time that school districts have gone to the extreme for inclusion of students with special needs; districts have overlooked the IDEA requirements of LRE. There needs to be a new set of standards for children who also need separate classroom help in addition to their inclusive classroom setting.

Throwing the Baby Out with the Bath Water

The core standards, assessments, and placements provide teachers and general education students with differentiated standards that students with special education needs require. We cannot make new practices without first considering the laws that structure the success of children with disabilities. It is of utmost importance to have children included with their general education peers and help them become successful in a mainstreamed setting. However, a tenet of IDEA states children need to be in the LRE, which means that children with disabilities need to be educated in a general education classroom to the maximum extent appropriate with their peers. LRE is not fulfilled when all children with special needs are included in a general education classroom without consideration for their disability. Children with special needs have the right to separate class time with the special education teacher to receive the assistance that they are not getting in the general education classroom. Their IEP specifies a time frame where they receive instruction in two classroom settings. Moreover, to *then* require these children with special needs who are included in the general education classroom to abide by core standards from a general education perspective, does not consider their special education diagnosis. Children labeled special education have their own standardization. Because we know and believe *strongly* that offering opportunities for children with special education needs to be included and mainstreamed is important, doesn't mean we now disregard the original diagnosis, goals, and objectives for their successful education.

Most children labeled learning disabled, emotionally disturbed, blind, hearing impaired, and physically disabled can be successful in a general education classroom receiving the additional assistance from a co-teaching practice. However, unlike those groups of children, many children diagnosed with special education needs in the area of autism, or multiple disabilities also need the extra classroom placement away from their general education peers. When school districts, state legislators, or education directors do not follow the immediate needs of these children, their education as outlined by IDEA may be put in jeopardy.

That is why it is mandatory to consider the special education standards that these categories outline and not be committed to full inclusion for all special education students. The categories from PL94-142 include children with types of disabilities such as orthopedic, emotional, learning, blindness, visually impaired, deaf blindness, intellectual deficiencies, developmental, deafness, hearing impaired, speech and language, traumatic brain injury, multiple disabilities, and other health-impaired disabilities. Each case is and should be determined on an individual basis. This makes certain that a child labeled with a special education diagnosis is given an opportunity for protection under the full extent of the law and the education their IEP decrees. America's educational system definitely needs core standardization, but we also need to check each child for specific goals and objectives that include LRE to maximize educational success. We cannot forget that children with special education needs require a definite and particular approach to reaching their academic, emotional, and behavioral level of success and accomplishment. We cannot neglect the commitments we have as educators to teach them among their peers, using the most appropriate methods, curriculum, and system for achieving success.

We need to establish a balance between what is *best* in an inclusive setting with what is also *appropriate* for that student, as well as all children in the general education classroom.

General education teachers need more training than they have been given in the past to work effectively with students who have special education needs, and more time to understand how important the student's IEP is to achieving success. The general education teacher also needs to know that co-teaching or collaboration with a special education teacher is *not a threat or a challenge* to their teaching practice. Co-teaching is a comprehensive way to approach the needs of all children individually, and with the expertise of two teachers, children receive the most ideal programming for their specific needs. With the requirement of full inclusion, the co-teaching model is a positive way to meet children's IEP needs and assist in programming for greater achievement for students with a special education diagnosis. In this regard, schools are not discarding or ignoring what is essential for students' academic and emotional development. In addition, all children benefit from any introduction of new approaches to increase their reading skills or other content-area skills.

Anything teachers can do together will benefit special and general education students. A true inclusive class can be advantageous. The IEP *must be* an integral part of the student's schooling.

Lessons Learned

- Teachers and administrators really need to pay close attention to the philosophical view of how reading is taught when traditional approaches fail. The lesson is to have the courage to say **NO** to traditional approaches and research.
- Identify alternative approaches that have new paradigms and new philosophical views of how children—especially those with disabilities—need to learn.
- A new paradigm or basic set of assumptions we believe about reading and how children read is needed before innovative practices, procedures, programs, and curricula will have a positive effect. Children will become readers and increase their comprehension when we begin to understand that their personal knowledge helps them increase reading skills.
- Parents had to unite in protest across the country in order to receive public school access for their children who were handicapped.
- It takes the commitment of many to make significant changes. Even when the U.S. government wanted to reverse the law, parents stormed Washington and made sure the public law was honored and children with handicapping conditions were allowed to be educated with their peers.
- Arrange a level of standardization based on something other than an educator's beliefs about what they think children should be able to learn. Look at a continuum of skill levels. Perhaps even structure a different evaluation piece that has children's input. Children are smarter than we think.
- General education standards are not appropriate for measuring the academic or behavioral talents, skills, or weaknesses of children with handicapping conditions. The effectiveness of the legally mandated IEP helps these children achieve at their own level.

- All children need core standards, but children with special education needs have their own standards through the IEP process. Children's academic progress is based on differentiating standards, which means that teachers are constantly thinking of reinforcing children's strengths while acknowledging children's weaknesses to help overcome them.

- If we as educators would become more sensitive to what children with special education needs can do, we would be able to incorporate their standardization into the core standards. We need to be cognizant of strengths as well as weaknesses of all children and teach accordingly.

- Children with special education needs want to be included, but the circumstances for their inclusion should be based on the strengths they have and how they will feel as a cohesive part of the class. We must be cognizant of how all the children in the classroom respond so children with special needs *really* feel included, accepted, and valued.

- When we do not consider the opinion of the children, we may place them in situations which may be more detrimental than if they were mainstreamed. When these decisions are made without children's input, the result may be an uncomfortable situation for special needs children. Understanding that we also need to ask them and determine the best class placement based on their desires, helps facilitate the children's success.

- When teachers work together in an amicably collaborative way, the children model the teachers' behavior and attitude toward the children with special needs. Children learn from what they see and hear. Children learn from what they experience.

Summary

When the educational system learns to trust parents and teachers and practice the standards that were devised for special education children, *everyone* wins. Acceptance is the primary purpose for children adhering to the core standards which are infused into their IEP. When they achieve their IEP goals and progress academically, there is a stronger relationship with an inclusive classroom. Special education children are provided with experiences that enhance relationships with their peers, and general education children learn acceptance and feel community and camaraderie. Core standards for children with special needs should be applicable for only the areas where children can appropriately function in this setting.

Chapter 5

Teachers Share Their Power and Help Children Accept Their Own Power

Jake was frustrated with reading and other academic subjects. When his grandmother brought him to me she was afraid he wouldn't want to participate in my reading program. He didn't get along with his teachers or many children in his school. He didn't like reading and didn't feel any success in academics. However, when she mentioned to Jake that she wanted us to meet and that I could help him to want to read and that reading would be easier, he was willing to meet me. I began speaking with him and he told me how frustrated he was because his teacher didn't recognize his academic strengths. Although he was in fourth grade, he was given extra time because the teacher thought he could only do first-grade work. During our session, he was very attentive, explaining things he really loved. He agreed to take my reading test so I could set a beginning-level reading score; a reading level reached when he answered all the comprehension questions correctly.

When we began the reading session, Jake was so fascinated by the thesaurus that I told him he would receive one before all of the sessions ended. (My usual time for gifting the children with a *Roget's Thesaurus* is during the last session.)

As he began to write his first story, he was so interested in sharing his experiences that time just flew. During the third session, I gave him an additional thesaurus for his classroom so he could share how to use it with his classmates. I had an ulterior motive for doing this. I wanted his teacher to know how resourceful he was, and to *see* his potential for completing age-appropriate academics, especially in the area of reading. After I gave him the second thesaurus, I asked if his teacher allowed him to share it with the class. He replied no. I then asked why. Jake told me his teacher said the book would be too difficult and there was too much the class had to do with daily requirements, so there was no extra time to give him. I was not only disappointed, but I felt his rejection, too. We continued with our sessions and Jake became happier as he learned to read. His grandmother talked about his interest in reading books at home. Even his behavior changed. He became less frustrated during school. He made two significant changes after successfully completing **You Read**. First, Jake started to read books that were above his grade level, and second, Jake took the standardized school assessment where he achieved the highest score in all areas of reading, with a 100 percent in vocabulary and reading comprehension, when he had previously scored below basic level in all areas of reading.

It was my interest to share my experiences with teachers and parents, as well as administrators who may be absent from the classroom. I wanted to give children with special education needs opportunities to be empowered. When a teacher tells them there is no time to share what they know, it is counterproductive to the learning process. I have learned in my many years of teaching that you *never* degrade or humiliate a child, either publicly or privately. A teacher should also be cognizant of what is said to special needs children because these statements sometimes stay with them for life.

We need to share our power with children and let them teach as *we* become the learners.

There are many effective approaches teachers use to enhance the lives of children and this chapter brings a recognition and appreciation for what teachers do and say that present a shared power between them. It is also an acknowledgment of how to accept children, particularly children with special education needs, become the *real teachers* in your classrooms. There are many ways to empower these children to understand they have potential to be successful. Even children who have more than a mild disability can strive for their own successful accomplishments.

I presented some techniques and suggestions for parents and teachers to recognize the strengths and talents of children with special needs. This chapter addresses specific ideas and recommendations that are related to the content children are learning. Many children have skills that are not recognized as viable because they do not learn them in traditional ways. General educators can use children's hidden skills as assets to enhance learning for all children. Acknowledging their skills helps them feel included as they improve academically and socially.

When the paradigm is changed, teachers can acknowledge that children in their classroom have knowledge in subjects that teachers may not have. Teachers need to tap into that knowledge recognizing that children have the ability to self-educate. Teachers should approach learning as an opportunity to share the content of a subject and as an invitation to involve children who have the knowledge base to share what they know. When teachers enable the child with special education needs *everyone* changes.

When teachers share their power for information and knowledge, they enhance their own skills and learn more deeply: when you teach, you learn *twice*.

When children learn their knowledge can be something that someone wants, they feel empowered. They can show leadership qualities, but they need to be given a chance to excel and contribute to the classroom. Most of the time children don't get that chance because of their disability. We need to change the perceptions of how they are treated and empower them. When teachers share their power with students, a synergistic energy develops between them and it shows the potential that students have brought to the forefront.

How Children Become Teachers

Although teaching is a set of skills, every human being has the capacity to teach. An important factor needed to teach is to share one's passion. Even though some people have a single vision for their area of expertise, they may not show an interest in other subjects.

Your children can *teach*. You just need to be patient and accept the things they want to teach you. A story about a second grader comes to mind. As a teacher supervisor, I was helping a second-grade teacher engage her children during a science lesson. The teacher's edition textbook specified the children had to learn about flies. I wasn't even interested in flies, so I assumed the children wouldn't be interested either. As my intern teacher watched me, I taught the class how to brainstorm by telling them *they* would choose the insect we would study that day. The top three insects would be chosen, and from that list students would choose one. I was teaching them a skill they could use for the future, as well as recognizing how important their opinion and choices meant to the lessons. The children's first choice was the cockroach. Oh, my heavens. I was not happy. What changed my attitude was Kyle, the child with learning disabilities. He raised his hand and said, "Cockroaches are my favorite insect. I know everything about them. Do you want me to tell you what I know?" I responded quite quickly with enthusiasm. "Wow, could you really tell us about cockroaches?" A dialogue began, as Kyle said, "I tell my mom all the time, so she's sick of hearing about them." I brought Kyle up in front of the class and he proceeded to explain what he knew. The teacher watched me write down some facts. I only stopped Kyle to tell him the class would do a unit on cockroaches that he would lead, so I didn't want him to tell us everything that day. I had him help me give assignments to the class. He felt proud. The teacher received a call from his mom that evening and asked her what she had done to motivate Kyle. He had come home from school filled with excitement that he *taught* the class all about cockroaches. I was so appreciative. The teacher told his mom that she was trying a new approach to her lessons and that the class chose to study cockroaches for their science unit. Since Kyle knew so much about cockroaches his contribution was an added benefit to the class. The change in Kyle that carried over to other subject areas during the school day was such a refreshing outcome. Kyle's attitude about doing his work also changed.

Children need recognition from various sources, but recognition from teacher and peers is often more important than from parents.

Sometimes teachers need to share their teaching skills in the classroom. Children have ideas that can be shared and even applied to curricula. If their ideas are sincerely acknowledged, it may help teachers find other resources to offer the class. Teachers are often reluctant to share their skills especially with children with special education needs. They may be unsure of how children will respond to a child with special needs. The most important shared quality for both the teachers and children with special needs is trust. Earlier I spoke of the need for teachers and parents to show their authenticity to their children.

Teachers need to show their authenticity to all children, regardless of whether or not they have special needs. When teachers allow children to "be in charge," they are showing their authenticity in the classroom, giving children an opportunity to learn from their knowledge. When teachers admit they don't know something, but are interested in any child in their classroom researching a subject, it adds to their authenticity. The teacher is not giving the child an assignment, but rather enabling the child to be empowered by offering knowledge.

Children with special needs feel valued when teachers ask them to share their knowledge.

Children can become teachers throughout the school day. When children answer homework assignment questions or participate in a classroom discussion, they teach. However, this approach, which has been a daily procedure since the beginning of schooling, is not a shared process. The process begins with self-confidence children have toward a certain subject. I have found that children can be natural teachers as long as they feel confident about a subject. When others ask them to share what they know, there is a tendency for them to feel pride, so their response to sharing is usually positive. But they also feel more self-assured when asked to share their knowledge.

Why It Is OK for Children to Know More Than the Teacher

There are several reasons why children with disabilities know more than their teachers as it might relate to certain subjects. The most important reason is that knowledge is meant to be shared, and children are like sponges that continually absorb everything they see, hear, feel, and sense. According to Piaget, an infant has an awareness that is carried throughout childhood experiences and an interest in sharing knowledge. Generally, teachers are taught that it is their job to share *their* knowledge. B.F. Skinner[9], known as the father of behaviorism, was the first psychologist to promote that learning was a behavior that children received primarily from their parents and teachers. Teachers were taught to present material that children needed to learn. Skinner promoted the belief that teachers are responsible for the curricula and teaching objectives to ensure that students receive the correct information. Within this philosophy there was no recognition that children had knowledge to share. In the 21st century, educational philosophy has changed to include a more holistic learning approach which acknowledges children's abilities that focus on more interaction with the teacher.

The structure of reading has become more child centered and the publishing companies of textbooks, especially the books for literature, emphasize inclusion of multicultural characters and real-life situations.

---

[9] B. F. Skinner, *About Behaviorism.* (New York: Vintage Books) 1976.

The need for this change is grounded in the changing demographics of the country. As more immigrants from Asia and the Middle East were settling in the United States, the need to reflect on the diversity of the changing population was evident. I suggest that it may be more powerful for teachers to call upon children in their classrooms to share their knowledge about subjects that are relevant to curriculum objectives. In the same way I described how Kyle was able to share his knowledge of cockroaches; teachers can call on children to research topics and share what they know. Children *enjoy* being called upon when they have something to share. Every child likes to *shine* in the eyes of his teachers and if he can tell people about what he knows, the opportunities for respect from his peers are special, especially if he is perceived as disabled in the classroom. Children in the classroom are happier when they feel recognized in a positive way.

An example of knowing the importance of children's knowledge is reflected in my experience teaching fourth grade. I was teaching a physical education class and noticed that children with special needs were always chosen last. So I changed the rules and gave children with learning disabilities the job as team captains. The two captains knew exactly who the better players were and classmates were yelling to be chosen. These team captains were now in a position of leadership in the eyes of their peers and were respected as having knowledge. That day my view was changed on building relationships. I chose to invite the team captains as leaders in other classroom activities, which really altered the attitudes of the children and dynamics of the classroom. I noticed new respect for the students with special needs by their peers.

If we took my example and used it as a measuring stick for acknowledging the strengths of children with special education needs, we might have less bullying and more camaraderie among children. I believe that we need to set a positive example for all our children. Showing them how they can be an asset to others is very important. Remembering that children have a great deal of information, and knowledge to share gives them the reason to believe that they can become teachers. If we choose to share our specific knowledge we can assure children that their knowledge is essential because they have purpose.

Why It Is Important For Children to Become Teachers

Once we accept the premise that it's alright for children to know as much or more than their teachers regarding certain subjects, we can answer the question of why that is important. Psychology reports that we all strive to be in the stage of Abraham Maslow's[10] self-actualization level of development. That means that we have achieved a high degree of success and comfort and are really aiming to give of ourselves to others. This level of development recognizes human beings' personal fulfillment, personal growth, and self-accomplishment. Usually problems, whether they are learning or behavioral, are emphasized and children are not recognized because of their special needs. These types of children are usually not recognized for *any* strengths they have. Consequently, if teachers find a subject these children know, teachers could be *advocates* in the classroom, providing children with disabilities the opportunity to share what they know. Robert Brooks[11], a Harvard psychologist, discusses his research and thoughts in his book *Raising Resilient Children*. He emphasizes the importance of acknowledging and appreciating what children with any kind of handicapping condition can offer, as their knowledge is a contribution to share.

It's important for children with disabilities to become teachers because when humans share what they know, they empower people who receive the knowledge. I once asked a friend what lessons are learned when children have disabilities. He responded by telling me that lessons are learned for the individual with the handicapping condition, and anyone that is associated with that person. Understanding that concept helped me to consider choosing my slow learners as team captains. Many choices I made as a teacher helped me to empower children with disabilities who were students in my classes.

When you give a child with a disability the freedom to teach, everyone learns—*even* the teacher.

How to Look for Changes that Help Children Become Empowered: Recognize That Change is Constant

We are all in the flux of change. We accept changes in our own lives looking forward to recognition from others. Yet, we may have difficulty looking for positive changes in our children with special

---

[10] Abraham Maslow, *Motivation and Personality*. (New York, Harper Publisher) 1954.
[11] Robert Brooks, *Raising Resilient Children*. (New York: McGraw Hill Publishers) 2001.

education needs. Since the children's IEP has been the basis of standards for their achievement, it is wise to follow what has been written. The IEP meeting includes parents or guardian, teachers, administrator, school psychologist, school nurse, and speech therapist that convene to structure children's objectives and goals for their education. These goals in the IEP represent the weaknesses and approaches to help children improve their education. A significant difficulty with IEPs is that they are based on children's weaknesses— not strengths. Because each child's IEP is individual according to his or her needs, there isn't flexibility for acknowledging or building strengths that each child may possess. One sign of change is to recognize that the goal or objective may be written below the child's level of ability. That doesn't mean that the child is going to meet the objective every day, but the response you and other teachers receive from the child will tell you if the objective is too easy or too difficult.

Another way to help empower your children with special education needs is to discuss their IEP goals with them. You might confer with your entire classroom, but the questions that you ask the child with special education needs will be related to his or her IEP goals.

I have emphasized the importance of practice, structure, and application for curricula to be child centered. Many requirements, standards, and general education school objectives promote child-centered values, but they do not apply child-centered practices. Decisions made by teachers and administrators that stress child-centered curricula are really asking children to participate, but not to be leaders. The best example of children being empowered is when they *know* and *believe* they are in control. When teachers allow children to be in charge, they become empowered.

An example of empowerment is to include asking children for their assistance. When teachers observe a child with disabilities misbehaves, they might request the help of that child as a resource, providing information for the rest of the class. Instead of a reprimand, the teacher could provide a purpose for the child to behave appropriately, which might change the way the child responds. A teacher's request for assistance might be the motivation for the child to be empowered, changing negative behavior.

Looking for opportunities to help children with disabilities actually demonstrates they can be empowered and will change the way they view themselves and how they are viewed by others.

Learning is an Active Experience: Promoting the Experience Results in Children's Learning

Although we know that learning is an active experience, we sometimes overlook the results. To further explain, it is important to discuss an "active" experience. It is essential that children be an equal contributor toward the content and organization of what teachers are teaching. I am suggesting we change the paradigm, or what we believe about how children learn, and change the way teachers approach curricula.

If we don't have a voice in what we are teaching, we don't feel invested in the process or the outcome. It's alright to have a boss tell us what we need to do, but if we have knowledge and information about a subject or process of how the task is handled, we want to be an integral part of that process. If adults are left out of the process, there is not eagerness to achieve satisfaction about the work being accomplished. We need to have that same kind of involvement in our classrooms and our teachers need to have the same kind of role in involving children, as managers have in the workplace. This process and new assumption about children will change the way teachers teach.

As a teacher, look beyond what you think children with disabilities can do and promote what you know are their strengths that will empower them.

Currently, because America's schools are emphasizing test scores and preparing children for taking standardized tests, teachers are not given the opportunity to *teach* children. They spend so much time teaching "to the *test*" that the relationship between knowledge and learning is driven in a direction separate from the *real* learning process. The components of learning include using tacit and explicit knowledge. Michael Polanyi[12] believed that we know more than we can tell. We need to recognize that children with learning disabilities also know more than they may be allowed to tell.

Even children need to have an investment in the outcome of their education. Therefore if we accept a new paradigm, explained by

---

[12] Michael Polanyi, *The Tacit Dimension.* (Chicago, IL: University of Chicago Press) 1966.

Thomas Kuhn[13], we can change the way we present information and what we believe about the process of children's learning.

Learning is not a passive process. Sometimes it appears that teachers are giving information to children and expecting them to retain it and use it.

The metaphor of "banking education," according to Paulo Freire[14] describes how teachers fill up the heads of children so that they can learn the material the teachers teach. The problem with the paradigm of assuming children come to school to learn whatever they don't know, is that children are already learned beings, and have their own knowledge to share. Real learning develops from direct involvement with children.

Real learning allows children to *actually teach* the information that they have learned, regardless of where or how they have acquired it. When children learn, they also teach. The *art* and *act* of teaching is an experience that enables children to have someone else positioned to be the learner. So the purpose of education, as an active experience, not only involves children as participants in the process, but engages teachers as *learners*. We must accept a different paradigm in order to reason that way. I use the children's knowledge and understanding of their world and their passions as the foundation for teaching them to read. The theory is based on the holistic way of learning and enables children to engage in learning by teaching what they know. While they share what they know, **You Read** also introduces writing as the basis for reading.

The process of engaging children in this way is the practice of changing their behavior and attitude about themselves. Therefore, when children with learning disabilities experience **You Read**, they are internally transformed and understand how important they are and the knowledge that they bring to our lessons. The process is collaboration and we work together to get the best results. The results are not restricted to their reading improvement alone, and they also start to develop a positive self-concept, acknowledging their own strengths.

Learning comes at different times for different children. This is similar to how we are exposed to technological information.

---

13 Thomas Kuhn, *The Structure of Scientific Revolutions*. (Chicago, IL: University of Chicago Press) 1996.

14 Paulo Freire, *Pedagogy of the Oppressed*. (New York: Continuum) 1970.

Remembering that we learn in unstructured incidental ways, there needs to be recognition and appreciation of what children bring to the learning process. All of us are exposed to information constantly throughout each day and need to understand that children experience the same kind of exposure. If we give them opportunities to share the information they have, we will empower them, and possibly change their behavior and the way they respond to us in a positive productive way.

Lessons Learned

- All children need acknowledgment, but when we are influenced by the politics of education and don't listen to our intuition, we are missing the time to be learners. When we take the moment to listen, we help children with special needs set an example for children without special needs. Our lives as teachers are more enhanced, while enabling the special needs children to share their knowledge.
- When teachers and children share knowledge, it promotes independent learning.
- When teachers take time to recognize how much each child can contribute to the classroom, they influence the learning of everyone in the classroom. The willingness to be a learner, as well as a teacher, will give children an opportunity that they may not have had in other settings.
- Children with special needs want to feel accepted and recognized for their knowledge, but they want to be asked because they still question whether others would care about what they know. We all want to be asked; it makes us feel worthy of sharing.
- Children want to be called upon to share their knowledge. They will feel a sense of pride to know that what they have to say matters.
- Give children a chance to excel, sharing their strengths so they feel empowered. It also gives teachers an opportunity to learn more about what children can do.
- Making assumptions about the abilities of children with disabilities can contribute to children's low self-esteem. Let them show you the range of their capabilities and have them rely on you to recognize and support their efforts to overcome weaknesses.

- When we say that curricula and lessons are child centered, we *practice* what we say. By *inviting* the child to contribute to the content knowledge, we give the child an opportunity to be a resource of information, gaining respect from children and adults. A holistic approach changes the child and may change the child's behavior.

Summary

This chapter focused on the teacher's relationship with the child with learning disabilities and highlighted important concepts which identify ways that parents and teachers can assist children to become more successful readers. There is a need to help parents initiate responses from their children with problems so that they will feel empowered and strengthen their confidence in their own skills. When we are asked for our opinion and feedback about a subject, we feel worthy about the knowledge we have. Human nature tells us that we want to be accepted for who we are and acknowledged for our strengths.

As educators we need to embrace a new paradigm that practices children's life experiences as part of a child-centered curriculum. Children with learning disabilities need to believe that they are accepted by their peers, and by the professional education community. When we embrace a holistic paradigm, we educate the whole child and emphasize what he or she needs as each one learns about passion for subjects. To embrace a holistic paradigm, we will have a different type of child with special needs attending our schools and living in our homes. They will truly be empowered and know their strengths and talents and can make a contribution in a positive way.

Chapter 6

Oral Vocabulary is the Foundation for Learning to Read

Bruno was one of the students I taught in Juvenile Hall in San Diego, California. He was detained for 120 days in the facility. He really didn't lack the reading skills the other boys had, but needed some advanced reading skills to build his vocabulary. When I met him he was somewhat agitated because he was required to take my class. We discussed furthering his skills and advancing his reading abilities, especially in vocabulary and critical comprehension. He shared with me his passion for playing guitar and writing lyrics. He explained his interest in writing love songs and requested his sessions be directed toward that goal. I was willing to comply because I knew after the first session Bruno didn't have problems reading or comprehending. He just wasn't interested in learning the traditional way. I also knew I could help him extend his skills and teach him new strategies.

*The first activity with which we engaged was learning how the **Roget's International Thumbed-Index Thesaurus** worked. The Thumbed Index doesn't work like an alphabetical list of synonyms. The book contains 325,000 opportunities for learning or using new words. Bruno was so fascinated by the book he asked if he could have it right then. (Typically, I give the thesaurus to students once they complete my program. This way they have not only used the book in my sessions, but they can practice what they learned on a daily basis. This technique ensures continued success with their writing.) I told him I would get one for him, but in the meantime, I asked him to look for the thesaurus in his detention center library.*

I saw Bruno the next day and as we began writing lyrics to his new love song, he asked me if I knew what the word predilection meant. I had not heard that word used often, especially by young people. (Now it is one of my favorite words to share with my students). He said he found the word while looking through the thesaurus in the detention center library. He wanted to know what word rhymed with predilection and I told him he could use any word that ended with "tion."

He was so focused with learning new vocabulary, he told his dorm supervisor how many new words he was learning in his literacy class and two significant changes occurred at the detention center. The first change happened during daily breakfasts. The youngsters that held a group meeting after breakfast instituted a word of the day to learn from the thesaurus and use throughout the day. Bruno was recognized

73

in his meeting group as a leader and asked to teach the new words to other juveniles in his dorm. The second change happened at study sessions after dinner. Once a week, Bruno would share his new vocabulary words with his dorm mates so they could increase their vocabulary. The most significant result observed by the teacher was Bruno's attention span. He significantly improved his homework assignments and concentrated on what he was learning. His teacher at the detention center had never seen him so attentive, focused, and caring about his academics. Her expectations of him changed. He now would be recognized as one of the top three students in her class.

The Importance of Vocabulary

Vocabulary is significantly important because infants learn vocabulary by hearing words. Babies babble, mimic, and experiment with sounds and learn words through trial and error. They are not *taught* to speak; babies listen and repeat words they hear from others. Sometimes children need guidance as they experiment with new words.

Children are introduced to words with regularity and are continuously learning the meanings of these words. The beginning of a child's vocabulary is developed in the home, in the child's surroundings, and as part of a relationship with family. As children begin to speak in full sentences it is also a natural process that they know the words and the meaning of their sentences. Vocabulary building continues as a lifelong skill. Evolving technology has also given children an opportunity to advance in reading and vocabulary because they are exposed to new words every day through the Internet. Reading material on the Internet introduces children to new information and research at the click of a mouse.

Children's vocabulary increases daily. As a parent or teacher, you want to introduce children to new words and reinforce the use of them.

Vocabulary is inadvertently built because acquiring oral language is a natural process in a child's learning. Even children who have difficulty reading are attracted to learning new words. One example stands out. Jasmine was a first grader who spoke English as a second language and was learning to read. She was participating in **You Read,** and I asked her how she felt about a story she had written. She replied she was happy. I wanted to introduce her to several words from the thesaurus that were synonyms for happy. Jasmine chose the word *jazzed*. When I asked her why, she laughed and said it was *fun* to say.

In the structure of the program, writing comes before reading, so children practice writing their words and sentences with a passion for learning new words. The reason writing comes *before* reading is the basis for **You Read** which relies on children's oral-language vocabulary. Since the research data has supported the premise that children have a 25,000-word vocabulary, their oral vocabulary helps them learn to read. Vocabulary is the impetus to reading and understanding the written word.

The more words children learn, the greater their vocabulary and the more effective their speaking and writing skills become.

Experiences are the Foundation for Building Vocabulary

Parents should provide as many experiences for their children with learning disabilities to set a foundation for exposure to words and new vocabulary. Children need to be in a safe environment so that they can feel comfortable admitting they don't know a word. We are not always certain that our children understand the meaning of words they use. My experience has shown that the majority of the time, children use words correctly. Oral language is required for almost everything children experience. Take advantage of every experience to expose your children to new words.

New situations enhance vocabulary. Every opportunity to carry on a conversation is a basis for building vocabulary. Parents should also engage their children in conversations where new words and concepts are introduced. Young children can always learn from their older siblings.

One experience that parents and teachers can provide is a "round-table" discussion, also known as a forum, with all members of the family or classroom participating. When arranging a family meeting, be aware that your children can challenge a family member to explain his or her position; what the adults and children say cannot be dismissed, but can be questioned and verified by the challenger. Often adults have a tendency to dismiss what children say. Children's voices need to be heard and recognized for their knowledge. I have emphasized the importance of *listening* to your children. I want to stress the importance of listening and creating the round-table discussions so your children can have a venue to express themselves.

Children become involved in their own dialogue with siblings. These dialogues may center on subjects such as school homework, socializing among peers, or asking an older child for advice. Even though children may not want parents to participate in those conversations, parents can speak very candidly with their children. These conversations are helpful when learning new vocabulary words, but the discussions can also assist children with problem-solving and comprehension skills. Everyone in the family must understand that regardless of the content of the conversations, learning is *always* happening for everyone and that dialogue of *any* kind is advantageous.

Learning through conversations enhances all the members of the family. Children need continuous conversations with family members to share their knowledge and learn new information.

Children Can Teach Us and Improve Their Vocabulary

To illustrate how beneficial children are as teachers, I'll describe an eighth grader, Ryan, who had difficulty doing his work. As the oldest in the group, he boasted about being in charge of the classroom because he had attended this school since first grade and he knew how the system worked.

After his insistence to take over the classroom, I decided I needed to have individual conferences with all my students during that first week of school. I believed each child needed to know something about me because I was new to the school and had different rules than the previous teacher. Ryan inspired my talk, but I wanted students to know I cared about them and what they thought was important for learning in my class. I met with Ryan first. That was the beginning of Ryan's transformation. I asked him what he liked and what was important to him related to school and school work. I explained that all of us had strengths and weaknesses and I emphasized the need to help each other. I told him about my difficulty moving furniture and placing things around the classroom. I noticed he was shaking his head and said, "Don't worry, Dr. Stone, I will help you move furniture." I knew at that moment that he would not be a problem in my class. He continued and said, "I will be your assistant and be instrumental in helping you when you need me." The word, *instrumental,* I believe he knew and I was not surprised when he spoke about his willingness to help me. That conversation changed both of our lives. Ryan became my first peer tutor, and after requesting to help my third-grade student, he became motivated to complete his own work.

Several days later Ryan's homeroom teacher approached me and asked how he did so well on his English essay. The vocabulary words he used even surprised his homeroom teacher. He became attentive in class and was better behaved. What had I done to motivate him to work and complete the assignment? (Ryan had never completed an assignment for the class.) I told his teacher about our talk and how he became a peer tutor for my third grader who needed help with his multiplication tables. Ryan became motivated to do his school work, and knew he could succeed because he felt respected. He became a resource for the other children and was never late for my class because he knew it was his responsibility to introduce new words to the students. Ryan was a valuable asset to the beginning of our day, and he thrived during the last year of middle school.

Children have the ability to share their own vocabulary. Allow them the opportunity to shine and be in the spotlight.

Oral Vocabulary Builds Reading and Comprehension Skills

As toddlers learn to talk to their parents or family members, they are likely to have bedtime stories read to them. As children are exposed to books, they are receiving the preparation for reading skills. Oral vocabulary builds reading skills. Parents can prepare children for successful reading skills even before they receive formal lessons by introducing them to the comprehension of the stories rather than by introducing them to letters and sounds. There is a need to help children understand what they are reading since the purpose of why we read is to gain information. Whether that information is for entertainment, gaining knowledge, or some type of recreation, we read to know. Once children know or have knowledge, they can participate in verbal and written activities throughout their lives. It is important to teach them how knowledge is gained from discussions with others. But if the children have questions or a difference of opinion from what others say, they need to be able to read additional information to make informed decisions about what they have been told. We are constantly in conversations that require us to research whether or not the information is accurate. Consequently, it is better to teach children about the meaning behind the stories than specifically about the letters and sounds.

Even children's picture books that are short stories can be discussed to help children comprehend the written word. When parents or family members read storybooks aloud *before* children begin to read, they can ask what they think the story is about. They can discuss the pictures to see if the children can predict the story line. After the story is read and the children know what the story is about, the adults can ask how they might change the story ending. These types of activities prepare children for comprehending stories and teach them critical thinking skills *before* they ever get to a formal school learning environment.

Teachers question children's ability to comprehend reading material. Often thought processes are lacking because children don't have the experiential background to critically think about situations. I have found that even my university students who read technical material don't know how to question what they have read and be discerning, astute, and selective regarding the accuracy of information. We have not taught people to question what they read. I am *not* saying that all written material is not accurate or worthy of publication. However, on occasion an article or written research may have inaccuracies; we need to be diligent not to accept everything we read. We have a right to question, as you have a right to question what I have written in this book. When people question, they learn. When children question, they also learn.

Building Vocabulary

When children participate in reading groups, reading centers, or free reading time, they continuously learn new vocabulary. This new vocabulary can be reinforced at home playing a variety of games. The first game I love to play with children is concentration. For example, 5x8 note cards can have the word on one card and the definition or synonym on another card. Children match the words with their definitions or synonyms. In Chapter 1, I explained how affirmations are introduced to help children feel accomplished and have a strong sense of self-confidence. You also can use affirmations as a forum to write your child's new vocabulary word. Games teach children strategies that have potential for improving not only children's vocabulary, but also children's knowledge. In addition, children can get together outside of class and play these games so they can teach their peers new vocabulary words they are learning.

Learning vocabulary and meanings of words helps children understand what they are reading. It is important to choose reading material that is age appropriate.

In your home you can create a word wall that is similar to your children's school classrooms. New words can be written down and added to the wall on a regular basis. As you or your children introduce new words, provide a synonym or very short definition. Also make sure children write a sentence that contains the word. Often you will be aware that your children already know the meanings of these new words, which can be connected to any of the concepts they are learning in school.

One of the most important aspects of learning is the coordination of using information learned at school and reinforced at home. It is necessary to involve your children in informal ways to learn concepts and understand what they read.

When your children learn, they can also teach.

There are several ways to build vocabulary as children learn new information through listening, engaging in conversation, and sharing knowledge. I recently met a four-year-old who is a good conversationalist. She knew words from conversing with her parents and was not shy about talking with me. She commented on my various rings and complimented my glittery, shining ring as she said how plain my other rings looked in comparison. Even at four years old, she was observant and very descriptive about what she liked and what she found plain. This is a typical example of how children's vocabulary expands through their exposure to words. They intuitively know the meaning of these words and they can use them in a proper context.

The task of parents and teachers is to be cognizant of how children converse. Building children's oral vocabulary as they speak is the foundation for reading and helping them to be skilled in comprehending material they read. Building vocabulary is directly related to comprehension.

The interrelation between oral vocabulary and reading skills contributes to proficient reading and comprehension skills. It is very important to emphasize to children who have difficulty reading that just because one can read the words on the page doesn't mean one knows how to read. Reading is the process of understanding the words on the page and the meaning behind what the sentence, paragraph, chapter, and book convey. Some children are classified as *word callers*. They know how to *phonetically* read the words, but they do not know what the sentence or paragraphs means, and are unable to describe the characters or details about the story they have just read.

Children think they are reading because they can pronounce the words and even read smoothly or fluently. However, they don't understand the story and it needs to be explained. They tend to mask the fact that they don't know what they just read and cannot answer even the simplest questions. Children may have very strong phonemic awareness; they know the sounds of the letter combinations but it doesn't ensure that they understand what they read or even know what the individual words mean.

Children can sound out words very successfully, but they do not necessarily have an understanding of what they have read.

Lessons Learned

- Children's vocabulary is the basis for their reading skills and therein lies the potential for them to learn new information.

- Introduce a new word to your children every day to increase their vocabulary.

- Every individual experience that children have results in learning new vocabulary. Sometimes children don't realize the extent of their knowledge, but as adults we need to reinforce our children and help them see how effective their oral language can be in facilitating new words.

- Provide a forum for children, especially those with learning disabilities, to shine and be in the spotlight. It will be a positive change for them and us.

- Teaching children how to be discerning about the material they are reading and evaluate that material gives them an opportunity to be critical thinkers and participate in discussions as they gain knowledge and information.

- Learning is enhanced through games and activities that inspire children to be teachers. We are all teachers when we share information.

- Just because children can read words or may have strong phonics skills does not guarantee that they understand what they read. There is a very significant difference in reading words and understanding what the text is communicating. Be aware that when children say they can read, they may not comprehend what they have read.

Summary

Children's experiences are the basis for developing vocabulary and providing opportunities for successful reading. Parents and teachers, as well as siblings and peers, can also support their development of vocabulary. In addition, children are exposed to many situations for them to be informed, or inform others, regarding learning new vocabulary. Children have an intuitive sense of knowledge and use that knowledge to learn new information. The primary objective of teaching reading is to expose children to situations where they are given opportunities to share, learn, and teach.

The idea that *to teach is to learn twice* gives children a chance to be empowered, to share what they know, and to improve their reading and comprehension. Vocabulary building doesn't need to be based on specific lessons since children are learning new words on a regular basis. Parents can take advantage of family situations, experiences, and opportunities to provide children a chance to expand their horizons and become expert readers. Remember that reading is the comprehension of the written word, explaining what the story is about, making judgments about the story, and enjoying the experiences the author is sharing. Help children practice new words, challenge them to use new words on a regular basis, and empower them to know how important their knowledge of vocabulary will make them proficient readers.

Chapter 7

How to Be an Advocate for Your Children

Charles was a frustrated ninth grader who was a non-reader. Like many of my students, Charles was intelligent but underachieving. He could remember and retain information; however, he did not show appreciable progress. He did have an additional problem: he had a speech impediment and couldn't pronounce certain words.

Charles had desperately wanted to read because as he said, "Important things are found in books." If he could read better, he said, he could learn how to put a motor in a car, diagnose a problem related to cars, and become a mechanic. I knew he was intelligent, but I was having difficulty understanding him because of his ability to enunciate. During one session I asked him if he ever had speech therapy. He remembered he went to Children's Hospital when he was very young—he emphasized the word "young." I talked with his mother who explained that his speech therapy sessions ended when he entered kindergarten. Children's Hospital suggested he continue speech therapy in school, but he only received sporadic sessions in kindergarten and subsequently was dropped from speech therapy.

I recommended to Charles' mother that she request a meeting with school officials and have him tested for speech therapy. She knew he needed speech therapy, but the school had never followed through after his year in kindergarten. She told me many people had trouble engaging Charles in a conversation because of his poor pronunciation. His difficulty with pronunciation wasn't restricted to conversational speech, but also affected his reading fluency.

I strongly believed in advocating for Charles and volunteered to attend the meeting with school officials that I suggested. I chose to help his mother advocate for him so that he would receive speech therapy. I explained what she needed to do and outlined several steps to present in the meeting. Although I supported her during Charles' first meeting, she was prepared and confident to speak on his behalf for subsequent meetings. She learned how to empower herself and get the necessary school assistance for Charles. Realizing how powerful that was for her, I decided to share my suggestions for advocating.

Parents of children who have learning disabilities need to be aware that the special education law IDEA protects parental rights so their children can receive *all* the services available. Parents *must* take an active part in their children's meetings and sometimes initiate those meetings with teachers, administrators and anyone who has interest in their child.

Advocacy is a process that promotes protection of the rights of any human being. Parents need to know that they have the power to be involved in their children's education, and can help make decisions about their education. Talking to teachers and administrators is a developed set of skills that can help children succeed. Sometimes the authority of teachers and administrators can seem intimidating to parents. When children are having difficulties at school, they are most likely having difficulties at home. Open communication with parents helps children achieve positive results in school. It is very important to know that teachers and administrators respect your knowledge about your child. You know your child better than anyone and need to feel comfortable as an advocate.

Personal Support Group

Many parents don't want to admit their child has a problem or needs help. When the problem is made known, it becomes an opportunity for advocacy. As a parent, you want to do the best for your children and offer them everything they need to enhance their lives. If you were looking for a piano teacher, a sports coach, or an art teacher, you would research the best candidates. As you learn to ask for what your children need, you are also teaching your children how to become their own advocates.

The first step is the acknowledgment of the problem, and then discussing the available resources by inquiring what assistance the school can provide. The next step is seeking additional help with the assistance your child is receiving in school. Seeking outside help should be comforting. When you speak to friends or neighbors about your child's reading problems, they may feel comfortable in sharing that their child might have problems. That kind of sharing can result in a personal support group for problem solving.

Personal support groups are a valuable resource to learn what other parents are experiencing and trying to understand. Sometimes children's ADD is fueled because their reading problems are so pronounced that they begin acting out in the classroom out of frustration. It is true that children's behavior isn't always influenced by their academic frustration. Over the years I have observed children change their behavior when they become successful in reading and other subjects.

When parents meet others who are experiencing similar frustrations, there is an acknowledgment that helps them believe they can help their children overcome reading difficulties. People involved in the welfare of children need to become engaged in solutions to help them succeed. It is the willingness to share with others that helps parents recognize that their children's difficulties are similar to other children.

It is not a negative reflection to admit your child has difficulty reading or with other academic or behavioral struggles. You will help your children and yourselves by sharing their obstacles in reading and literacy.

The Advantages of Being an Advocate for Your Child

As an advocate for your child you are seen as a person who is a contributing member of the IEP "committee" suggesting goals and academic objectives. When you approach teachers from a position of being proactive, you send a message that you will take an *active* position in your child's education and you want to be informed if plans change. When you present yourself as an advocate for your child, teachers will be more informative and contact you regularly to report your child's progress. As an advocate you will also be asked how to help your child in the classroom. Teachers will reach out to you because of the knowledge you bring to inform them.

Even parents who don't believe they have the knowledge base that teachers have will be able to contribute to their child's education. It is *undeniably* an advantage to be an advocate for your children. There are benefits to you, but there are stronger benefits to your child.

You know your child and his or her level of achievements. As an advocate, be *insistent* that your child should or should not participate in a school-related activity. Many opportunities are presented throughout the day for your child's involvement. If you are realistic about what your child can achieve, inform the teachers. However, ask your child. If your child wants to try something, *allow* it.

Parents tell me teachers hesitate to expose children with disabilities to experiences where they may fail. We all know that failure is a part of life and the importance of failure is learning that people can overcome it as they understand what they are experiencing. Parents, teachers, and administrators gauge how much they believe children with disabilities can handle. Children have an innate feeling of what they are able to do.

There are many circumstances that children with disabilities face, and adults in their life are hesitant to give them a chance to attempt tasks and succeed. There is usually an assumption that children are unable to handle the tasks and will fail. The advantages of being an advocate are that you have a deeper sense of your child's capabilities and you can share that knowledge with school officials.

I was very proud of a child that I taught when she actually became her own advocate. In addition to having learning disabilities, she had cerebral palsy—a physical abnormality that caused her to have great difficulty walking. But she wanted to spend more time in the regular education classroom and went to the school psychologist to arrange her own IEP meeting. The psychologist was surprised, but the law states that *anyone* can request an IEP meeting for *any* reason. The special education law covers the rights of parents *and* their children, which is under the due process section that protects parental rights in all meetings and gives parents permission to request what they believe is good and appropriate for their child in the regular education classroom.

You know your child better than teachers and should be involved in your child's educational programming.

It may be necessary to educate parents on the process of advocating for and encouraging their children to be their own advocates. When those lessons are learned, it seems to be in the best interest of the children to understand their rights and communicate their wants and needs through arranging their own meeting. As of this writing, there are no courses or seminars that teach parents how to be advocates for their children. Some websites have suggestions for parents. What usually occurs is that parents *find* advocates that are very expensive, but know how to navigate at IEP meetings. An IEP meeting is held after the child has been recommended for special education assessment and parents have signed legal forms to approve of that assessment. After testing is completed, a school meeting is called to discuss results of all the testing and whether the child qualifies for special education services. Those attending that meeting may include the school psychologist, the principal or vice principal, special education teacher, speech and language specialist, school nurse, parents or guardians, regular education teacher, and sometimes the child.

When children of at least eleven years old attend the IEP meeting, they seem to have a vested interest in their education and how they will get the individual help they need. When children are present, it also conveys a commitment among the committee and an added respect for the child. If the child qualifies for a special education placement after a deliberation of the assessment results, a decision is made about how much time the child needs to spend in the regular education and special education classrooms.

The importance of having children participate in the meeting is their agreement as to what type of academic help they need and how they intend to work on identified weaknesses. The student has input into his or her own educational program and becomes part of writing educational objectives. When children and parents are an integral part of committee decisions, they become proactive in the education process.

Although time and placement decision procedures have changed over the years, to give parents a better understanding of that process, the committee decisions have always been to serve in the best interest of each child. It has always been the objective to place children with special needs in a general education classroom with their peers for as much time as possible. Consequently, the time and subject matter needs are the responsibility of the special education teacher, and children are removed from their general education classroom and given extra help in another location.

However, after many years of looking at that model of removing children from placement with their peers, school districts today have become aware that children need to be exposed to a general classroom setting. Some school districts have advocated a co-teaching setting where the special education children are kept in their general education classroom and the special education teacher co-teaches with the general education teacher. Special education teachers have their own student group in the general education classroom. The classroom becomes a foundation for mainstreaming and developing relationships among *all* children. By exposing children with special needs to appropriate behavior, and arranging activities so everyone in class can participate, the co-teaching arrangement can set the stage for children becoming advocates for each other. Children without special needs are supporting those with special needs.

I was pleased to see a high-achieving child who asked me if he could partner with a peer with special needs for our class field trip. They liked the same sports and watched the same television programs. This was a *different* type of advocacy related to a new friendship, and they continued their friendship in other settings.

We need to recognize the need for children with special needs to engage in friendships with all children. It helps promote acceptance.

Advocacy for parents during the IEP meetings may be an ongoing activity because sometimes after the committee decision is made specialists don't follow through with the recommendation for services. The advocate doesn't have further association after initial services are provided. Consequently, parents must now advocate for their child themselves. At times an outside advocate returns or parents call the school to arrange a new meeting to discuss why the child isn't receiving the services scheduled to receive. But when the advocate returns, parents are obligated to pay for the advocate's time.

When parents learn their child isn't receiving services, they can file for due process. The procedure of due process occurs when either the parent or school district are not pleased with services to the child. The subject of that procedure is making certain the rights of the child are met and that the school follows through with what it agreed to offer the child. The procedure of due process was established to ensure parents had complete control over the educational rights of their child with special education needs.

Your position as a parent advocate is to receive the best, most appropriate and least restrictive environment (LRE) for educating your child, while being part of a regular education classroom. LRE is a term that is instituted to protect all children with special education needs and is the center of understanding how children are placed in the proper special education classroom. The basis for LRE is to make certain that special education children spend as much time as possible in their regular education classroom receiving assignments with their peers. Placement decisions for the child attending a special education class are made during an IEP committee meeting. However, when the committee considers LRE they focus on how well the child will be able to adapt and participate in activities with their peers.

The reason it is so important for the child with special needs to be included in the committee meeting is that he or she can tell the committee about feeling included in a particular subject. Occasionally a child tries to participate in an activity when the adults are unsure of achievement levels. The committee also becomes familiar with the temperament and security levels of the child. Children with special needs want to be included and accepted. If they remain in the general education class, more often they are seen as part of the class and there is significantly more integration with their peers.

Be Honest with Your Knowledge of Your Child

School officials are hopeful that parents take an active part in their child's education. Parents still need to be the guiding force for their children's academic progress. Parents know their child *better* than anyone. Teachers are with your children almost every day for seven hours and have only a minimal understanding of the manner in which children respond to the teachers. You can provide missing information about your child's mood and behavior at home. More than likely if children are frustrated at school they bring those frustrations home and vice versa. Having regular conversations with your children will also help their teachers.

Parents and teachers are usually on the "same page" when they are working for the good of the children and their success. The goal is the same for parents and teachers who need to realize they are on the *same team*. They bring their *own* knowledge and expertise to children. While honesty about what they know regarding strengths and weaknesses of children is important, it is also *critical* to include the child in the discussions; the child must be included in the plans or programming of his or her educational future. Children also see a united front between teachers and parents, when they can agree on what is educationally best for the children.

Honesty will assist the teacher in planning positive reinforcement as well as consequences if a child misbehaves in school. Parents can inform the teacher about their child's behavior at home and determine consequences or reinforcement at home. It's important to attend teacher meetings when possible to give parents and children a chance to be informed. Balancing the responsibilities of family and work,

89

meeting with your child's teacher, and sharing your insight will confirm commitment.

The more honest you are to your children and their teachers, the more committed their teachers will be in helping your children succeed.

Parental commitment is one of the most important factors in helping teachers understand a child with special needs. I urge parents to communicate with their children's teachers because they *need* the information parents can share. Sharing is also advocating for your children. For example, if your child has a frustrating morning, emailing or sending some kind of communication to the teacher will help the teacher respond more knowingly that day. Since every day may be different, it would be beneficial to send a note or email when your child has had a good morning, too.

Adults tend to emphasize children's weaknesses and don't spend enough time acknowledging their strengths. In Chapters 2 and 5, I wrote a segment on authenticity and how important it is to be authentic when speaking to your children. That concept also includes being authentic when speaking with your children's teachers. When you show teachers you are authentic, they know you are committed.

Your Child Can Achieve More than You Think

As your children's advocate, you can emphasize what programs and school services they need and the achievements they have made. The significance of those achievements helps your children strive to reach their highest potential. Even children with learning problems need to believe in their ability to reach for long-term goals that show their potential. Children with disabilities often times have strengths in sports, music, and creative arts.

Scott, a child that had difficulty reading, was articulate and his artwork was one of the finest drawings I'd seen from an eleven-year-old. I spoke frequently with his mother, who wasn't as excited about his artwork as I. When his mother came to visit and saw Scott's work displayed, I surprised her and called the principal into my classroom, because he also admired Scott's work. That incident helped motivate Scott to try harder and he achieved more than he even thought he could. Scott's mother was amazed and acknowledged his artwork by displaying his drawings at home. My relationship with her changed following that visit. She began to send the artwork he produced at home to school, and we had an exchange of notes on a regular basis. She began to acknowledge his strengths. I noticed that Scott's self-confidence improved, and his classmates began to recognize his artwork, too.

Advocacy is Emphasizing Your Children's Strength

The meeting with Scott's mother also changed the attitudes of other students who believed in their ability to achieve. Once they were encouraged, they had a different attitude about school and their potential to achieve. The recognition for children with learning disabilities needs to be continuous. An authentic acknowledgment of children's strengths has a dual purpose. First, it reminds parents and teachers that in spite of any disabilities, children have strengths in *something*, and that something doesn't need to be related to academics. Second, when children are authentically identifying their own strengths and being saluted for those strengths, they often change feelings about what they are able to achieve. This change can transform them into believing they can be successful.

When children become their own advocates, they see how their passions and knowledge can help them become who they really want to be.

There is an increase of reported bullying in schools and an awareness of children being tormented among their peers. When parents and teachers act as an advocate for children, they can help to change the adverse treatment children are receiving from peers. Teacher and parental attitudes can also change the way they help their fellow classmates recover from bullying. Children inadvertently learn to advocate for each other.

Children in my intern's middle school class experienced advocating for each other, as well as themselves. After an introduction to my four classroom rules for managing children's behavior, **My Turn, Be Kind, Voice,** and **Rule of 25**, they realized they could be assertive when they were speaking and interacting with each other. **My Turn** is recognition that when a child or adult speaks, everyone in the class listens. If there is disruption the person talking stops and says, "It's my turn." **Be Kind** is a comment that children in class say to their peers when anyone says something mean. **Voice** is a word used when anyone in the class is shouting or talking loudly and others can't hear their peers. (The Voice rule is usually used during class projects when all the children are talking at the same time.) **Rule of 25** is a catch-all rule that is used when any child is misbehaving. If a child is making any kind of noise or commotion, the child is addressed with **Rule of 25** (the number changes depending on the size of the class), and he or she will stop the commotion. These rules were practiced by the teacher and children. For example, a student named Chad spoke to answer the teacher's question. Students were talking over him and he stopped, turned to his classmate, Javier, and said, "It's my turn." Javier stopped talking and said, "I'm sorry, Chad." During a physical education class, Jessica heard George make fun of John. She looked straight at George and said, "Be kind!" George spoke to John and apologized. As students learned that it was important to provide a safe atmosphere where they could interact without making fun, they began to learn about respect for their classmates and defended them. The result was a decrease of bullying and the class recognized their strengths could help them excel and help others.

Children *need* guidance but don't always know how to show others that they want it. We *can* stop children's self-destruction by being *aware* that they are calling out to us; we need to observe the signs and *listen*. The adage "go with your gut," is more than a saying. We are given instincts to help us know what is best for ourselves and for our children.

Parents as Lawyers

Parents are instrumental in their child's education and need to remain an advocate requesting services and being part of a collaborate team to help their children with learning disabilities succeed. I use the metaphor *parents as lawyers* because lawyers negotiate for their clients. When parents *actively* participate and engage themselves, they can obtain services their children need. These services may include a particular program that is written into their educational plan, more time to complete a test, or having a friend take notes for them in class.

The most important trait any parent can have is the openness to ask questions of any member of the IEP committee. The dialogue between parents, teachers, and administrators will be a critical factor in planning the best education for their child. Parents don't need a law degree to learn how to negotiate. What they do need is the *interest* to come forward and be an advocate in helping their children. When parents speak out for services, they set an example for their children to follow.

Shonda had much difficulty walking, but she was very smart. Her physical condition did not affect her ability to speak clearly and articulate precisely. She also knew that she could talk to me about anything. She told me that the teachers were treating students in the special education class in a demeaning way. She didn't like it, but didn't know what to do. I told her the next time the teacher talks in a demeaning way, she should raise her hand and comment saying it isn't nice to speak in a patronizing manner.

The example of Shonda's advocacy helps to illustrate the importance of empowering children and teaching them to be straightforward about how they should be treated. Parents and teachers need to stress the value of children with handicapping conditions becoming their own advocates and sharing their views and opinions about their rights to respect in spite of their limitations. Parents and children who become "lawyers" will see a change in the relationships they build and movement in their lives as being leaders in their families, schools, and communities.

Lessons Learned

- Parental rights need to be acknowledged and can only be emphasized if you present yourself as your child's advocate. To empower your child, you can be an example by speaking with teachers on your child's behalf.

- When you share the struggles your children have, you learn that there are people who have solutions that may help. It should not be embarrassing to be honest about helping your children. The lesson is to model good strategies so you can give your children the opportunity to learn from you. Sharing their struggles will empower them to be their own advocates.

- Advocacy doesn't need to be from any outside source. If parents take initiative to stand front and center, school officials won't seem intimidating. Parents can also teach their children to take the initiative to speak up for themselves and receive the education they desire.

- Children can be empathetic and caring. When we teach children how to be advocates, they rise to the occasion.

- Honesty is a value that can be *taught*. While you have in-depth knowledge of your children's strengths, there are still things *you* can learn. Talking with your child keeps you informed of any changes in their interests, which you may share with your child's teacher. Trusting your children and their teachers will enhance the honesty and trust you build with both.

- Setting an example for your children means "stepping up to the plate" and being an equal partner in educating your child.

Summary

It is important to teach your children with disabilities to stand up for their rights, to receive the education they need, and to be contributing members of society. When children learn that they have abilities and skills, they believe they can be productive. Teaching your children how to be their own advocate will help them get what they need. For example, some children have been able to arrange an appointment for their own IEP meeting and have given educators an agenda of what they deserve to have regarding academic help. Make it a priority to provide opportunities to assist these children. It is very important to make sure your children are aware that they have rights as well as responsibilities to advocate for themselves. You will not always be available to advocate for them. Once they learn to be their own advocate, they will also have confidence in the future.

Chapter 8

Using Information Technology
as an Effective Tool for Literacy

Nathan was an underachieving sixth grader who was below grade level in reading and had difficulty in understanding science and history. His mother came to me because she had had a conference with his teachers and they wanted to retain Nathan. (I believe that children should not be held back after the second grade.) I suggested Nathan work with me to build his literacy skills to overturn his teacher's decision. Nathan is very bright but didn't believe he had the ability to become a reader. The school district would administer a test. If Nathan showed no improvement, he would be held back and repeat the sixth grade. After discussing the test with Nathan's mother, the district did not indicate alternatives other than retaining him. When Nathan took the test after completing my reading program, he believed he showed improvement, but because of his lack of confidence, he wasn't sure. His mother told me the teachers were shocked. They reported that he not only improved, but he scored at grade level. The teachers decided not to retain him. That was good news for Nathan and his mother. **You Read** *was a program that worked and it helped Nathan gain confidence and the willingness to believe in himself.*

Nathan's story really doesn't end there. I was speaking with a colleague, Dr. James Jaurez, who knew that Nathan had accomplished so much through the program and he wanted to know why my program wasn't part of the digital age, utilizing computers as an effective tool for literacy. Dr. Jaurez provided me with a laptop computer complete with a writing tablet and stylus for taking notes. I immediately knew that Nathan would be a perfect candidate to use it. Although he was finished with the reading program, he was excited about writing another story using a computer writing tablet. After he wrote his story on the tablet, he could read it orally and also record his voice and set up a file to save to the tablet. When I attempted to explain the process, I discovered that Nathan already knew it. My immediate thought was to provide this opportunity for all my reading students. What a unique opportunity to use technology for teaching children to read and to write their stories for playback! **You Read** *includes children's writing as the impetus for reading proficiently.*

How Information Technology
Can Provide a Better System for Literacy

Reading programs for school-aged children have been developed and used in classrooms to improve children's reading and literacy skills for years. Information Technology (IT) has added a new dimension for children to develop phonemic awareness[15]. Technology incorporates a multisensory approach to learning to read with the visual picture of the sounds while children match sounds with letters. The use of computers as a tool to reinforce skills that children are learning in traditional reading curricula might be advantageous to replace the traditional reading approaches and make use of computers or current electronic devices in teaching reading. If teachers implemented the use of voice chips to replace the worksheets, children would get an interactive immediate response. Voice chips can imitate sounds for children to repeat and children can hear the correct sounds.

Information technology is only a tool to be used, *not* a replacement for teachers' interaction with children.

The recent IT development had a major impact on our lifestyles—specifically in the areas of communication, personal entertainment, and acquisition of knowledge[16]. Now widely used in education, IT has improved the teaching of literacy. E-books, the digital version of textbooks, bring new opportunities for learning and provide easier access to knowledge[17]. Margaret Elaine King-Sears recommended matching technology choice to literacy learning and cautioned against adopting technology for technology's sake[18]. Many teachers use IT as reinforcement after children have completed worksheets or teacher-planned activities. The goal of the integration of technology into

---

[15] Bob Lally, *Teaching Children to Read Using Technology.* T.H.E. Journal, 2001. 28(9): p. 56-57.

[16] Loui Nelson, Elizabeth Arthur, William Jensen, & George Horn, *Trading Textbooks for Technology: New Opportunities for Learning.* Kappan Journal, April 2011: p. 46-50.

[17] Lisa Guernsey, *Are E-books Any Good?* School Library Journal, June 2011. 57(6): p. 28-32.

[18] Margaret King-Sears, Christopher Swanson, and Lynne Mainzer, *TECHnology and Literacy for Adolescents with Disabilities,* Journal of Adolescent & Adult Literacy, 2011. 54(8): p. 569-578.

literacy lessons is to provide additional opportunities for learning to read. Instead of reserving multisensory approaches for children with learning disabilities, IT enables all students, regardless of their learning styles, to participate in the learning process. Children at any age can adjust and readjust to ways they learn as they engage in reading activities or exercises through technology. The IT systems can be innovative and reorganize platforms to specific needs of classrooms and individual students.

Specific Advantages of Information Technology (IT)

As we evolve in the digital age, it has been apparent that schools need to keep up with the changes. Many times teachers use computers as reinforcements, but teachers also need to receive professional development and are included as an integral part of the changes school districts are making. In Indiana, for example, the districts are conforming and restructuring using computer assignments, engaging students immediately during the instructional time. Children are investigating history and social sciences on the Internet and using analytical skills more precisely. There are software programs to assist students with writing. One specific program entitled, Dragon Speaks, actually transcribes what a user dictates. This software is one answer to children who have difficulty writing, but are very verbal and can express ideas orally. Lessons are now presented through teacher-created websites.

Information Technology devices open up an abundant potential for educators as instructional tools for literacy education[19]. There are many IT tools that have been created for preschool and beginning readers. These instructional tools have very simple directions and reinforcements and are colorful and fun.

Features such as text-to-speech as input and output, touchscreen, collaborating up-to-date information through the Internet, streaming videos, and high-definition photographs greatly enhance learning.

Since the development of these tools, researcher Laurie McDonald has called these children "digital natives," referring to a generation of children who are so familiar with computers and other information technologies that they don't have recollection of learning any other

---

[19] Gina Biancarosa and Gina Griffiths, *Technology Tools to Support Reading in the Digital Age.* The Future of Children, 2012. 22(2): p. 139-160.

way. However, McDonald also stated that education classrooms are not keeping up with the digital age of incorporating computers into literacy curricula, but instead are using computers as a reinforcement of class instruction. This phenomenon can also be described as connecting literacy and technology[20].

As teachers and parents, we need to keep up with these children who have computer knowledge at a young age called "digital natives."

What Does IT Provide for Special-needs Populations?

There are many interventions IT provides for children with special needs. Most specifically are the adaptive resources that children need, known to special populations as Assistive Technology. These devices include buttons and switches that a child operates in order to manually manipulate a computer. When children can't physically type there are optional devices that they can use. Assistive Technology includes hardware, software, and peripherals that assist people with disabilities in accessing computers or other information technologies. For example, people with limited hand functions may use a keyboard with large keys or a special mouse to operate a computer. Individuals who are blind may use software that reads text on the screen in a computer-generated voice. Children with low vision may use software that enlarges screen content. A text telephone (TTY) assistive device is for individuals who are deaf. Many county and state organizations provide a separate telephone number that can be connected to a TTY, so people who are deaf can respond to telephone conversations. People with speech impairments may use a device that speaks out loud as they enter text on a keyboard. Stephen Hawkins, a physicist with Lou Gehrig's disease, uses a variety of assistive devices to communicate and read through computer-generated appliances.

Updated technology that includes computers and current electronic devices has incorporated many applications (what we now call apps for smart phone technology) that support people with disabilities ranging from autism to visual impairment. One software program in the form

---

[20] Elizabeth Schmar-Dobler, *Reading on the Internet: The Link Between Literacy and Technology.* Journal of Adolescent & Adult Literacy, 2003. 47(1): p. 80-85.

of two apps is called voice-to-text and text-to-voice. Both can be uploaded to assist children with reading and writing. These new apps are a replacement for the Dragon Speaks program, which is still used but less popular.

New techniques for children with special needs enable children to click on their own apps and upload what they need. For example, a child with autism who has limited language now has an app for the communication of Picture Exchange Communication System (PECS)®, a board with pictorial icons that represent emotions, nouns, and any word that the child needs to communicate. The child uploads the app and chooses a picture or a group of pictures to ask a question or make a statement, similar to a child using sign language to communicate. This technology is a breakthrough for these children.

The use of technology makes a significant impact on children, especially those with special education needs.

How Technology and Literacy are Interconnected

Technology has been at the forefront of expanding children's literacy skills. Children can read without carrying heavy books and research information. However, children with learning disabilities still need the foundation of literacy skills to read the material accessible on the Internet and fulfill assignments that are computer-generated. Learning from computer programs that emphasize skills through playing games is a good approach to mastering some of those skills. Portable devices may be loaned to children to take home and practice their literacy skills. It is important to make sure teachers and parents are involved in children's learning regarding computer games so they know how their children are progressing and are available when assistance is needed. Mara was four and Talus was two years old when I met them and their parents during a gathering of friends and family. They couldn't sit still and were fidgety. After a while, their parents brought out an iPad® and an iPhone®. Their focus then immediately changed. It was amazing to see how quickly the children moved their tiny fingers to *turn* the pages and interact with the games they were playing. Technology has succeeded in capturing children's attention, and while they have independent learning curves, there is still a need for parents and teachers to supervise children's activities using computers.

When children are working with a reading software program, they need monitoring and reinforcement separate from the immediate positive reinforcement they receive when they answer a question generated by the computer.

Since computer-based reading games are also multisensory, they are a great advantage to children with learning disabilities. Games can be played with other children who have e-readers. Even though children have individual e-readers, they can still participate in classroom educational computer games.

In addition to games, using effective e-reading material can be taught to children with reading problems. Technology in the form of an e-reader device has the capacity to differentiate learning for children with reading difficulty. Curriculum has been designed for computer use through individual software programs. Children with disabilities are able to spend more time in one area of literacy as the software does not time out. The use of software with an emphasis on literacy has been created to consider different learning styles but must be monitored by teachers in the classroom. E-readers are available in the form of a Nook®, Kindle®, or an iPad®. E-readers help children self-pace so that they can receive their instruction independently. An e-reader is a tool that has been shown to be flexible in presenting material where children respond positively to the way the material is presented. If children have difficulty writing, they now can enter their information or answers to comprehension questions through a voice-to-text function. Prior to this technology, teachers needed to write or record the children's answers to a test or comprehension questions. More recently there is also an oral blog format where children can post their answers.

Computer-assisted programs have simulated teachers called tutors, who have been integrated into the presentation of new vocabulary words and reading material. These tutors are visually animated models that act similar to teachers. They present new words and give children instructions to repeat the words, while also reinforcing children's correct answers. Since computer-assisted instruction occurs in a one-to-one format, it does serve the needs of children with special education diagnoses. Computer-assisted programs are structured with a one-to-one ratio for instruction. Children work independently but have the feedback and support of classroom teachers.

Children are reading differently as they peruse the Internet for information. For example, what was traditionally taught as skimming or scanning a text is now performed in real-time to gain information to answer comprehension questions on the spot. Children are formally taught how to scan for information, or they develop the skills because they need to find the information quickly. They are able to navigate through many websites to retrieve information. It is advantageous to acknowledge new learning that is developed through media literacy. This new learning also requires differences in the strategies needed to use the information from the web.

Computers are a strong tool for increasing literacy skills, but teachers need to be present to monitor, answer questions, and guide students as they navigate through websites.

Group work is also structured differently and classrooms generally provide a computer, mobile device, or iPad® for each child. Children need to share computers or mobile devices if the districts are not prepared for the individual use. Considering the shift to technology as a new medium to teaching and learning, teachers and children need to be prepared for these changes.

How to Prepare Teachers and Children for Media Literacy

School districts need to make sure they provide training for teachers using computers, smart boards, and other mobile devices with regard to material that was previously written in textbooks or trade books. Some of the same traditional learning methods are applicable, but when children naturally engage in research and need to peruse many sources, they need to learn how to distinguish one source from another. Teacher- and student-training sessions must be ongoing. Children can be divided into buddies who help each other navigate through various sites looking for answers to comprehension questions, while analyzing the information and making sure it is retrieved for the assignment appropriately.

Classroom assignments using technology can have the versatility that was not found in the past. Since the access of computers and mobile devices acts as a reference instead of the sole source of information, children must realize there are Internet resources that are not applicable to answer their questions.

Another approach is to set up cooperative teacher teams in grade-level classes and have children work together on a themed project. Children help one another and share their own expertise on the computer websites. Some children are teachers as well as learners. Using computers and mobile devices in the classroom for projects allow children to show their skill and accomplishment in completing assignments.

As children work together to achieve the same goal—whether or not they have reading disabilities—there are strengths that they bring to help one another. Many times children with learning disabilities have knowledge about websites even though they struggle with reading the text. The use of cooperative teams of two or three gives all children an opportunity to excel focusing on their strengths. Their teachers facilitate the groups emphasizing the knowledge from each child.

As children venture off on their own using mobile devices, they are motivated to research information from their specific vantage point and contribute to the group answering questions, obtaining information to share, and learning more to increase their knowledge. Children with reading disabilities can be central figures in a cooperative group because of their contribution and focus on their passion. Computer access may be one of their strengths that can influence how the others in the group respond.

Classroom Libraries and Technology

There is a trend for trade books and textbooks to now be available in electronic form where children can access information through their e-readers and current devices. The library systems in school districts are changing and structured without call numbers or traditional indexing systems. Lisa Guernsey,[21] the director of Early Education Initiative at the New America Foundation, has reported that many more changes need to be instituted for children to regularly choose e-books to read. School libraries need to conduct training for teachers as the children begin reading more e-books. As libraries provide e-books for classroom use, there are various reading options for children with reading disabilities. One useful option is choosing to enlarge the print for reading by using tap and zoom and the option to highlight directly on the e-reader. Once highlighted, a menu appears and there are choices whether to know the meaning of the word, provide a synonym or tap on a sticky note to save the word.

Children can also use text-to-speech for reading aloud, which is an advantage over traditional books. Computer technology has advanced how children approach reading and research, and it has advanced their ability to scan text and answer comprehension skills. According to research, there are still districts across the country that need to change their library systems to give children more opportunities for reading books and conducting literature research on e-readers.

School districts are also providing classroom textbooks to children through e-readers. Districts are buying e-readers to provide new technology in lieu of heavy books. The same alternative reading options are provided for children as they read textbooks using e-readers or mobile devices. There are a variety of note taking options to mark important information from e-books. As technology helps change the way curricula is taught and learned, it will certainly add a component of depth to the process of how knowledge is acquired.

Technology and the Writing Process

This chapter has emphasized how various forms of technology have impacted learning, reading, and understanding text, especially for children with learning disabilities. Using all types of e-readers and laptop computers, the techniques of literacy instruction are becoming more versatile, allowing children with reading difficulties to be more successful. Now children with or without disabilities can benefit and gain reading skills as well as learn to enjoy reading because of technology. However, even with these advancements, there has not

---

[21] Lisa Guernsey, *Are E-books Any Good?* School Library Journal, June 2011: p. 28-32.

been an opportunity to incorporate the writing process into technology.

You Read has developed a way of using the laptop computer with the writing desk tablet and stylus to integrate the writing process. When children write their stories using the writing desk and stylus, they are able to read their story, have it recorded, and watch themselves reading. Children diagnosed with learning disabilities become successful readers after 14 days. Using the writing desk as a technological advancement, the computer keeps a file for children's stories and saves a video that they can watch.

The video file can be watched frequently. Children can receive feedback and feel confident the more they watch themselves and discover the process of reading is less stressful, more fun, and helpful to increase their literacy skills. It's an opportunity for children to see and acknowledge their progress as they move through the lessons of **You Read**. They also learn that watching themselves reading on a video helps them to monitor their improvement and motivates them to practice reading outside of the reading sessions.

Lessons Learned

- The use of computers and current electronic devices is effective in teaching reading and literacy to children with or without disabilities.

- Keeping up with evolving technology benefits children in general education classes and makes an impact on all children with special education needs. The use of technology can influence any child with a disability. Assistive devices promote independence for children with moderate-to-severe disabilities.

- Using a computer program solely for teaching reading skills is not practical. Reading software programs should be an added piece that helps children strengthen their skills and extend their learning. Computers can be effective tools and introduce children to new concepts.

- Computer games need to be reinforced by teacher-directed instruction and activities. Teachers need to be present while children engage in learning and navigate through literacy game activities.

- Teachers and parents need to trust children's knowledge of the sources they need to complete their assignments and be willing to have them be the experts. Teachers and parents also need to be supportive of technology information and engage in dialogue to learn and to teach. Technology can make a difference in gained knowledge, but it is only one type of tool in children's repertoire of resources.

Summary

There is no question that technology is beginning to be an integral part of literacy learning for children, especially those children with learning disabilities. As the educational systems integrate e-readers and other mobile devices, children will incorporate new material that their teachers have developed through classroom websites. Children learn how to navigate websites and their knowledge base increases as they read research on the Internet because the process is immediate and has a global network of material to be learned. Children who are "digital natives" are becoming more familiar with technology use as a free choice, choosing to use e-readers, and getting their information from the Internet instead of relying on traditional books.

Since e-readers have the flexibility to help the children with disabilities by enlarging and highlighting texts, children with reading problems *can* show an improvement in skills using e-readers. This improvement is seen quickly, and children's skill retention is stronger. Technology has provided an approach to substantiate the individuality of children with reading disabilities while helping them strengthen their reading comprehension and skill development, as well as their research skills on the Internet. To understand how technology contributes to reading success for children with disabilities, more support for teachers is needed. Teachers need to receive training and learn how the e-readers and technological advances can reinforce special education children's literacy skills. There must also be an understanding that technology is only a tool, and teachers and parents are needed to reinforce different approaches to reading. Both groups can learn from children who have developed a comfortable association with technology and can teach adults. With the rapid changes in information technology, we can look forward to the development of more advanced tools designed to support children with disabilities in becoming successful readers.

19945559R00068

Made in the USA
San Bernardino, CA
21 March 2015